FOAMSHIP

Shaping Organizational Success

R. David Bermudez

J.R. Lluberas

CONTENTS

Preface   i

The History of FOAMSHIP   v

1   Introduction   1

2   The FOAMSHIP Model   7

3   Finance: Generating Cash for Fuel   15

4   Operations: Creating Products and Services   29

5   Administration: Leading from the Helm   41

6   Marketing: Selecting Customer Ports   55

7   Souls on Board   67

8   Heading in the Right Direction   87

9   Innovation Drives Sustainability   101

10 Passage Across the High Seas   117

11 Conclusion   131

12 Appendix: FOAMSHIP Summary   137

13 Bibliography   141

14 About the Authors   145

PREFACE

"A ship in harbor is safe, but that is not what ships are built for."

John A. Shedd (Author)

Is management an art or a science? This is an age-old question that aligns with the debate over whether leaders are made or born. You will find many arguments on each side of the issue depending on whether you talk to executives, academics, psychologists, behavioral scientists, or philosophers. Regardless of whether your views of management are scientific or artistic, one thing is certain: as management, in general, has evolved, one sees in its execution the inclusion of many elements of the creative and inspired right side of the brain. Some management hard-liners would call that the "touchy-feely" side of management. However, if you look at most companies today, the obsolete notion of conducting "strictly business" without consideration to the individuals inside the organization has faded away, except in the most autocratic, old-fashioned companies.

Unfortunately, during challenging periods, a lot of the concern for the individual is thrown overboard. A challenging period could range from having a bad sales quarter and declining profits to growing too rapidly and not having enough resources to handle the growth. Such times can often result in management reverting to their old ways of doing business. Panic can cause leadership to return to basic survival instincts and toss away those things that they may consider unnecessary, irrelevant, or of no perceived value. This is when the culture of people being the most important asset can be lost.

With fewer people doing more work with limited resources, organizations barely have the time to help employees better understand WHY they do what they do, HOW it impacts the organization as a whole, and WHERE they are headed. Evolving since 1998, the FOAMSHIP model you are about to discover is the ideal guide for tapping into the collective workplace energy and enabling the entire "crew" to identify with the direction in which their

i

organization is heading. The beauty of the model is that it appeals to both those who are "clear-cut" about management, and those who are more empathetic to the needs of the individual. In other words, FOAMSHIP is the bridge between the art and the science of management within an organization. Organizational performance can then be seen in an entirely new light by business captains, officers, and shipmates.

First published in 1998, this revised business survival guidebook combines over forty collective years of work, study, research, and experience into an easy-to-follow-and-measure organizational performance model. We break the structure of an organization down into the fundamental business and human elements so that we can re-examine our work conditions with a fresh perspective and a shared point of reference: a ship.

Throughout this guidebook, we'll consider an entrepreneurial approach to management. Instead of viewing entrepreneurship solely in the traditional sense of "someone who assumes risk to start a venture", we'll be implementing a model that adopts the practice of entrepreneurial management within established organizations. This approach, commonly referred to as intrapreneurship, enables the innovative entrepreneurial mindset to permeate management practices at all levels within a diverse range of organizations.

No one in their right mind heads out on an adventurous sea voyage without suitable equipment such as a compass, charts, navigation equipment, foul-weather gear, life rafts, etc. Why then do some of us continue drifting along in our business lives; sometimes lost, sometimes dead in the water, or sometimes even sinking? The power of this model harnesses the collective intellectual and emotional forces present within an organization and converts visualization into entrepreneurial achievement. By helping the individual understand and focus on direction and execution, we can help to chart and navigate a new course for organizational performance.

If the concept of business-as-a-ship sounds simple, in theory, it is. However, in practice, it's a lot harder to implement and maintain successfully. In life, many seemingly simple things can be quite fascinatingly complex and complicated. For example, the mighty oceans cover three-quarters of our planet and are essential for all life, yet water is simply a combination of hydrogen and oxygen. Our very own amazing bodies are composed mostly of water and yet are intricate machines. The sun's fury is crucial for sustaining life on Earth, yet the sun consists primarily of hydrogen and helium.

Computers have revolutionized mankind and life as we know it, with little more than a collection of ones and zeros. Simple can be extraordinary!

To illustrate some of the points in this guidebook, we'll refer to real-life work practices gathered from exemplary corporations that began as entrepreneurial dreams. These examples depict our model's universality because they focus on the human element within any organization. Whether American, Asian, European, Hispanic, Middle-Eastern, or African, the human heart is the same wherever you go – it needs to belong to, and participate in, something bigger and of significance.

The idea of an "intrapreneur" is not a new one, however, the values and benefits associated with this mentality are often vastly underestimated. The concept relates to entrepreneurial behavior within established organizations. In light of today's economic turbulence and global challenges, exasperated by the COVID-19 pandemic, organizations from all sectors are being forced to find improved ways to operate. The FOAMSHIP model provides a dynamic framework for the sharing of information and solutions, as well as for creating stronger and more unified teams. Implementing an entrepreneurial ethos within an established organization can have substantial advantages.

This refreshing approach will give the organization's entire crew a new way of thinking as they embark on the adventurous undertaking of a business voyage. Regardless of your role within the crew, you will never look at your organization in the same light again.

So, grab your gear and head for the deck as we begin our journey aboard the FOAMSHIP.

Anchors aweigh!

~ FOAMSHIP ~
Shaping Organizational Success

~ FOAMSHIP ~
Shaping Organizational Success

THE HISTORY OF FOAMSHIP

"When all seems to be against you, remember, a ship sometimes has to sail against the current, not with it."

Matshona Dhliwayo (Entrepreneur and Author)

In 1998, the book entitled *FOAMSHIP: Navigating the Corporate Seas,* first introduced the FOAMSHIP model. 2005 saw the revised second edition of the book being released with an updated title - *The FOAMSHIP Guide to Building More Entrepreneurial Firms.* More than two decades since its initial conception, the FOAMSHIP model is still relevant and can easily be applied to today's business environment.

With years comes experience. The FOAMSHIP model was originally inspired by a failed attempt at a start-up company. Successful approaches to business and life have often been the result of previous failures, trial and error, and the hard-earned experiences of those who test the waters. This third edition of the FOAMSHIP guidebook incorporates the insights gained since the 2005 revision.

The foreclosure of a personal property, time spent on non-profit work, the creation of a successful contracting business in the US Federal market, a number of extraordinarily successful endeavors in middle of a pandemic, and a plethora of other real-life experiences have assisted the authors in forging a deeper understanding of how to thrive in life and business and achieve success in multiple fields.

The definition of success is subjective. The Western world's adoption of capitalism as the primary economic model means that it tends to equate success with financial wealth. However, there are many cultures where quality of life is believed to be the true measure of success.

As with most things in life and business, balance is essential. Regardless of how success is perceived by each individual, it will always be more

v

rewarding when there is balance. With that in mind, FOAMSHIP aims to provide a well-balanced path to success in all its various forms.

It's also beneficial to note that the FOAMSHIP model is not limited to business applications. The same principles can be used on a personal level to achieve a more rewarding and fulfilling life. When the right balance is attained and maintained, the journeys of both business and life are experienced more positively.

~ FOAMSHIP ~
Shaping Organizational Success

1. INTRODUCTION

"Twenty years from now, you will be more disappointed by the things you didn't do than those you did. So, throw off the bowlines. Sail away from safe harbor. Catch the wind in your sails. Explore. Dream. Discover."

Mark Twain (Author, Entrepreneur, Publisher)

Success in today's global business climate requires the consistent integration of many traditional and non-traditional business areas. These can include accounting, finance, operations, marketing, strategic planning, human resources, leadership, psychology, sociology, and ethics. However, helping organizations and people to clearly "see" and "feel" this integration in real life is no easy task. And that is the starting point of our voyage.

While exploring the many elements that come into play within a business setting, a lot of consideration went into how to focus this enormous mishmash of concepts into one unified picture – an "organizational mosaic", if you will. When viewing a mosaic up close, you're able to see that it consists of a collection of individual tiles. However, when you look at it from a distance, those individual tiles integrate to form a cohesive image.

Similarly, in any business venture, the alignment of people, processes, and purpose operating in unison is crucial. This is what enables the organization to function with clarity and execute its operations effectively. The FOAMSHIP model serves to bring the "organizational mosaic" into focus. Used correctly, it will assist each individual within an organization to understand their unique role and how they fit into the big picture.

The FOAMSHIP acronym symbolizes and expresses the core components of an organization.

~ FOAMSHIP ~
Shaping Organizational Success

"**FOAM**" denotes the fundamental "clear-cut" business areas of:
- **F**inance
- **O**perations
- **A**dministration
- **M**arketing

"**SHIP**" represents the less tangible elements of:
- **S**ouls
- **H**eading
- **I**nnovation
- **P**assage

Just as visualization has been proven to improve performance in sports, it's strongly believed that visualization enhances entrepreneurial thinking, and focuses the use of resources on the realization of business objectives. This led to the creation of the analogy used throughout this model. The eight organizational components above provide the structure and design of the ship on which we'll sail across the oceans of industry.

In essence, FOAMSHIP is:
A practical model to help captains and their crews visualize their organizational journey, and focus resources on the achievement of their shared goals.

Another important purpose of FOAMSHIP is that it assists in simplifying the complexities of business. An essential factor in doing so is to recognize and understand that the most vital asset of any successful organization is the human element. The FOAMSHIP model augments the crucial human-organizational link and improves communication between captain and crew. This, in turn, directs everyone's energies towards creating a more productive business experience. Additionally, it heightens the awareness that any individual action can positively impact any part of the organization.

Various analogy-specific terms will be used throughout this guidebook to support consistent visualization:
Ship – This is the metaphor used to refer to an organization, company, business entity, enterprise, corporation, or firm.
Voyage – A business event or activity. This could be a new business opportunity or venture, a special project, the introduction of a new product or service, or an innovative company initiative.
Captain – A person in a position of leadership who organizes, operates,

and assumes responsibility for a business venture. The captain is the Tactician who sets the vision that guides the ship. When considering start-ups and smaller businesses, this role often refers to an entrepreneur. In larger organizations and public companies, this includes executive positions such as CEO, President, and Chairperson of the Board.

Officers – These are the people who form the captain's immediate staff and execute the captain's orders to achieve the vision. Officers are the Technicians who set plans, establish procedures and control processes. This refers to vice presidents, managers, division managers, directors, senior supervisors, and other similar roles in middle management.

Shipmates – The team members within an organization who perform the actual work as directed by the officers. This typically refers to employees, but can also include contractors and any other parties who contribute to the organizational operations.

Crew – The crew consists of all the souls on board the ship who work together to achieve the captain's vision for the success of the organization.

Fran, a middle manager working for Bright Beacon Ltd., is an example of an Officer. In his role as a manager, Fran has to work at being the best leader he can be for the shipmates under his direction, while also meeting the expectations of Sam, the CEO of Bright Beacon Ltd. and Captain of the crew. The FOAMSHIP model helps to provide Fran with the skills and ability to successfully lead his shipmates and execute their captain's orders.

To help to navigate along this journey, the following icons are used throughout this guidebook:

A LIGHTHOUSE illuminates a significant point being made, where light is shed on a concept.

A SHIP reflects a real-life example of a FOAMSHIP concept.

~ FOAMSHIP ~
Shaping Organizational Success

A SHIP'S WHEEL represents FOAMSHIP benefits, which lead you toward success.

An ANCHOR grounds you with fundamental truths.

A COMPASS STAR indicates potential action items, or "to-dos", required to keep our ship moving forward.

A PULPIT is a lookout point that enables you to see where you've been and where you're heading. At the end of each chapter, you'll find questions to consider that will help you to understand and apply FOAMSHIP principles.

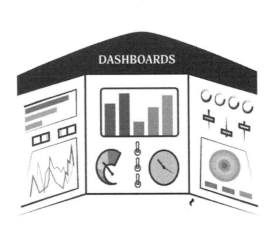

4

Throughout this journey another essential element will evolve as the FOAMSHIP navigates its passage. A ship's DASHBOARDS are crucial tools for any triumphant voyage as they measure Key Performance Indicators (KPIs). These metrics enable the captain to identify issues that arise, review goals and expectations, track progress, and monitor all aspects of operations to ensure peak performance. Dashboards for each business area combine to create an instrument panel that is critical to organizational success.

Next, we'll discuss an overview of the FOAMSHIP model to see how the entire ship is constructed from the eight organizational components.

Are you ready? Boarding has already begun and it's time to assemble on the Observation Deck.

Let's get going!

~ FOAMSHIP ~
Shaping Organizational Success

2. THE FOAMSHIP MODEL

"If you can visualize it, if you can dream it, there's some way to do it."

Walt Disney

The FOAMSHIP model utilizes the analogy of a ship to visualize the business journey and how to navigate it successfully. As can be seen in the illustration below, the structure of the ship itself is built from the four fundamental areas of business:

- **F**inance
- **O**perations
- **A**dministration
- **M**arketing

It's important to note and understand that these areas are shown separately only for illustrative and discussion purposes. In real life, these areas overlap and merge on a daily basis; sometimes even in turbulent conflict with each other.

With the organizational infrastructure in place, the less tangible elements which make up the rest of the model are:

- **S**ouls
- **H**eading
- **I**nnovation
- **P**assage

The FOAMSHIP model demonstrates how **S**ouls ensure they're **H**eading in the correct direction, using **I**nnovation to navigate a successful **P**assage.

~ FOAMSHIP ~
Shaping Organizational Success

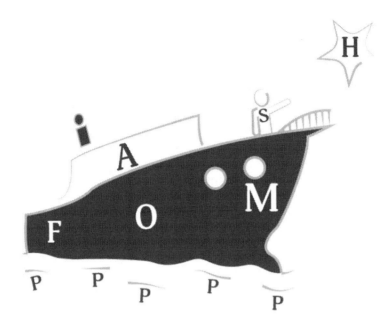

The FOAMSHIP Model

Symbol	Meaning	Description
F	Finance →	Efficient financial functions ensure the sustainability of the organization
O	Operations →	Optimum productivity and efficiency propel the organization forward
A	Administration →	Leadership and teamwork keep the organization focused on its goals
M	Marketing →	The compass directs the organization to relevant and beneficial client ports
S	Souls →	Individuals who make up the collective "spirit" which unites and energizes the organization
H	Heading →	The star represents the direction in which the organization is headed
I	Innovation →	Using information, skills, and knowledge to enhance the organization's ability to compete
P	Passage →	The sea represents the course the organization must navigate throughout its business voyages

~ FOAMSHIP ~
Shaping Organizational Success

<u>F</u>inance: The fuel we burn to drive the propellers

The effective and efficient generation and management of financial resources are critical to the success of any enterprise. Money is the fuel that powers the ship and how that fuel is managed will determine whether a voyage can be successfully completed. There is little room for error and a poorly selected venture or bad investment can leave an organizational ship dead in the water. Finance includes activities such as accounting, auditing, budgeting, cash management, tax planning, and investments.

As a manager, Fran is responsible for his department's budget, cash-flow management, financial reporting, and allocating financial resources to best serve the business goals. In his role as a Bright Beacon Ltd. officer, he has to provide his crew with the tools they require to perform their duties. But Fran also has to validate his department's spending to the captain, Sam, the company's CEO. To assist in keeping the propellers spinning, Fran must find ways to burn financial fuel wisely.

FOAMSHIP enables all crew members to become aware of their direct impact on and contribution to their organization's financial well-being.

<u>O</u>perations: The engine room of our ship

Regardless of whether an organization sells a manufactured product or a service offering, operations are the materialization of the business purpose. This is the core reason for the organization's existence. How efficiently the product or service is delivered depends on how well the resources are managed. The operations component includes elements such as physical manufacturing plants, design and engineering, inventory control, transportation, scheduling and fulfillment, and strategy.

Fran understands that operations are the ship's engines and that these must be in optimal condition to offer smooth sailing. To achieve and maintain a good speed and competitive edge, Fran and his crew must keep the operations running like a well-oiled machine.

FOAMSHIP helps us to determine whether our operations are running at optimum levels and or if a tune-up is required.

<u>A</u>dministration: The Bridge from which the captain and officers steer the ship

General management of all business areas, from the physical plant to the work environment, is included in the administrative function. Administration is the bridge, or command center, of an organization and it can face some tough challenges in keeping the ship on course. One of these is managing the interdependencies of all FOAMSHIP components.

Administrative duties within an organization are as complex as the instrumentation of a ship. Fran knows that no matter how sophisticated the instrumentation, neither he nor Sam can steer the Bright Beacon Ltd. ship alone. Managing the ship's speed and direction relies on teamwork. To be a successful officer, Fran must capitalize on his strengths and hire his weaknesses. Utilizing the organization's resources effectively will determine where and how far the ship will travel, so the crew needs to be united and focused on the business goals.

With FOAMSHIP, everyone is signed-up and "on-board" with the captain and the destination.

<u>M</u>arketing: Our compass - where are we and where are we going?

Marketing is what guides the destination of our ship to the most relevant and beneficial client ports. Grouped together under the category of marketing is everything to do with the sale of products or services, customer support and service, public relations, advertising campaigns, and social media.

Sam, Fran, and all shipmates aboard Bright Beacon Ltd. know that beating a competing ship into a customer port is crucial to meeting the business objectives. The crew also knows that the marketing team helps them to achieve this by guiding them to their destination and encouraging customers to choose their ship over others. The marketing crew ensures that customers are eager and ready to board the ship.

FOAMSHIP helps make our ship more desirable to our customers - the best one in the ocean.

~ FOAMSHIP ~
Shaping Organizational Success

<u>Souls:</u> All the individuals on board – whose energy is fundamentally vital

In recent years, many organizations have lost or even sold, their corporate souls. One of the reasons for this is because they did not value the souls of the individuals within their organizations. The concept of souls refers to the collective spirit and energy of all the people aboard an organizational ship. This concept is centric to the FOAMSHIP model.

Leaders, like Fran and Sam, need to understand that the fundamental energy source aboard their ship is its people. Without a shared desire to move forward, the ship will go nowhere. Therefore, a primary duty of both captains and officers is to cultivate, motivate, and harness the mental, emotional, physical, and spiritual energies of their crew healthily and positively.

A true FOAMSHIP organization has a healthy and vibrant collective soul.

<u>Heading:</u> The bright North Star in the sky - the organization's vision guides us to where we are headed

When undertaking a voyage, a ship sets its bearing and navigates in that direction. An organization must do the same by determining the direction in which it will be heading, and clearly stating this to all crew members on board. There is an old saying which goes: "If you don't know where you are going, any course will take you there." An organization is almost guaranteed to fail if it wastes fuel by sailing aimlessly without proper direction.

As the captain, it is Sam's responsibility to plot Bright Beacon Ltd.'s course according to the goals that are to be achieved. The vision and mission must be clear and precise in order to provide all souls on board with clarity regarding the direction in which the ship is heading. This ensures that all the efforts of the captain, officers, and shipmates are focused on where they're heading.

FOAMSHIP helps everyone stay focused on the Heading.

<u>Innovation:</u> The ship's information and communications systems support innovation

In a ship, the hull and decks provide the infrastructure to hold together

~ FOAMSHIP ~
Shaping Organizational Success

all the elements that provide the ship with the ability to navigate its course. Similarly, within an organization, the proper infrastructure enables the swift and accurate exchange of information and knowledge. The strength and agility of a business are impacted by how well that combination of information and knowledge is utilized to encourage and enhance innovation.

There have been times when Fran has felt torn between his own vibrantly entrepreneurial soul and his role as a manager within an established organization. However, Sam's encouragement of his ideas to create a more efficient work-flow has shown him that innovation has a role to play in all organizations. Whether as an entrepreneur or an intrapreneur, the development of new and improved methods, processes, products, and services is required for any business to grow and survive.

Sam and Fran understand that they need to promote smooth-flowing communication throughout the entire organization. This will support innovation, stimulate collective learning, help to avoid costly mistakes, and assist the organization in gaining a competitive edge.

FOAMSHIP drives innovation by creating a stronger infrastructure through better communication and information management.

Passage: The rocky seas and uncharted waters to be navigated throughout the voyage

There are many variables and external influences that cannot be controlled in business. The ocean represents the course the ship must navigate throughout its voyages and it contains many of these unknown and uncontrollable elements. This can include factors such as the economy, weather, customers, competitors, politics, global events, and acts of God. Ignoring signs and signals from the external environment can lead to failure.

Over the years, Fran has noted two key elements that are crucial to long-term success:

1. Preparation, and
2. Innovation

During times of crisis, such as the global COVID-19 pandemic of 2020, the importance of these two elements becomes obvious. In both life and

~ FOAMSHIP ~
Shaping Organizational Success

business, there are situations that simply cannot be predicted, and therefore, the amount of preparation possible is limited. To weather these unforeseeable storms an organization must have the ability to react intelligently whilst navigating its passage. Creative crews who take full advantage of technology, and any other tools at their disposal, are more adept at staying the course.

A captain and crew must be prepared to deal with and learn from any unexpected events which may surface during the voyage. Each new journey is unique and requires a different course to be taken to reach the desired destination. Along the route, each soul on board gains experience and this makes these crew members more valuable contributors to future expeditions. Both Sam and Fran encourage each individual to learn as much as possible from every venture. A seasoned crew will be able to deal with ambiguity, be flexible to sudden changes in the course, be eager and willing to share knowledge and new experiences, and be alert to impending dangers and potential opportunities.

FOAMSHIP builds an alert crew ready to sail any passage.

Next is a detailed discussion of each FOAMSHIP component. This will provide an understanding of how the FOAMSHIP model can be applied to your current organization or future venture.

~ FOAMSHIP ~
Shaping Organizational Success

3. FINANCE: GENERATING CASH FOR FUEL

"Happiness is a positive cash flow."

Fred Adler (Venture Capitalist)

It is generally the case that most entrepreneurs and intrapreneurs are driven by a passion for what they do, more than the potential monetary rewards. This passion enables the perseverance required to transform ideas into reality. In turn, this then fuels the motivation necessary to keep a ship afloat during times of perilous turbulence. The FOAMSHIP method can help captains, like Sam, to share their passion and vision with their crew. A shared vision will assist in realizing the captain's business dreams while generating greater profits ("fuel") along the way.

Money should not be the sole purpose of anything in life and companies can't operate successfully with a strictly financial mindset; not even financial institutions. When an organization concentrates on doing the right things in the right way, the financial rewards will follow. A timeless quote from the multinational consumer goods company Procter and Gamble (P&G), perfectly sums up this operational mindset:

"Profits are like health, the more the better; but it is not our sole reason for existence."

In addition to profitability, it is imperative to promote an environment of high ethical standards, excellence in brand management and advertising, superior customer service levels, quality products and services, reliability, and respect for the individual. To be a good captain, Sam must always bear in mind that the overall success of the ship is determined by the combination of the human and business elements.

At the stern of the FOAMSHIP model is Finance. It is the primary responsibility of Finance to effectively manage the fuel supply (cash) and

achieve the most efficient fuel economy for the ship. Cash management has a direct impact on the value of an organization. Finance manages cash by analyzing, allocating, and planning the use of all funds. Fuel must be burned to move the ship forward, but the fuel supply must also be replenished. The accumulation and usage of fuel supplies must be handled as efficiently as possible.

The Fuel Cycle

The following basic diagram illustrates the cash "fuel" cycle aboard the FOAMSHIP.

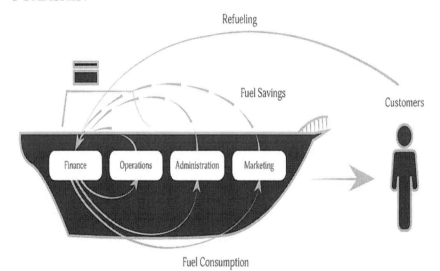

Fueling Our Ship

When considering new ventures, investors are external partners. These investors are typically equity partners or financing institutions, and they provide the fuel for the initial launch of the ship or a supplementary boost during the voyage. However, at some point, the ship needs to become profitable to repay the investors.

The ship invests fuel in all the activities and responsibilities that consume cash during the execution of business. Cash as fuel is consumed in the form of salaries, benefits, supplies, equipment, furniture, and all the other resources used to power daily operations. The consumption, or investment, of fuel differs for each component throughout the various stages of the business lifecycle. For instance, a startup would require a greater Marketing investment when compared to a mature and well-established organization.

16

Although the Finance shipmates are responsible for providing insight regarding the ship's fuel supply, all crew members need to work together to find ways to economize and save fuel. Reduced fuel consumption can be achieved through concise and practical operations, well-maintained equipment, streamlined processes, and innovative programs.

An organization's customers are the ones who fill the fuel tanks in the form of payments for services rendered or products sold. When the ship operates in a manner that keeps them satisfied, customers provide a continuous source of fuel for future voyages. If the organization's customers become dissatisfied with its products or services, they will pump their fuel into a competing organization instead.

An important goal for any organization is for the incoming fuel to exceed the outgoing fuel. This will establish an efficient cash "fuel" cycle that provides the ship with profits to distribute, re-invest, or retain in reserve for future rainy days.

Shipmates in Finance should provide insight into the financial well-being of the ship; the rest of the crew should always be on the lookout for cost-saving opportunities.

Sustainable Voyages

Today's environment requires organizations to look beyond their bottom-line profits. As a conscious captain, Sam employs the concept known as the triple bottom line. This involves also considering the social and ecological impacts of the business ship. Socially responsible activities result in contributing to the greater common good, as well as yielding financial benefits.

Similarly, operating with respect for the environment and conservation of resources is aligned with our shared responsibility to future generations. "Green" business practices no longer have the stigma of impeding the bottom line as they're increasingly providing financial returns as well. FOAMSHIP captains and crews strive to ensure that they sail across thriving oceans, not dead seas.

Turbulent Waters

No matter how well a crew is prepared for a business voyage, it is

inevitable that the ship will encounter rough seas at some point. The shipmates responsible for Finance need to be involved in analyzing the risk and rewards of particular navigational plans.

Financing, insurance, and bonding are all important elements of business that need to be in place to ensure that sudden bad weather does not affect the ship in a critically threatening manner. External influences such as an unexpected action by a supplier, subcontractor, or competitor can be mitigated by sound financial management.

The 2020 COVID-19 crisis is a prime example of an unexpected external influence that affected businesses and personal lives on a global scale. Such an unprecedented event cannot truly be prepared for, but a strong financial position can make the difference between survival and extinction – both professionally and personally.

A Team Approach

Finance shipmates assist the captain and the rest of the crew to maintain the ship by providing depth, breadth, and insight into the financial functions. Although a number on its own might be just one financial indicator, important questions can be raised about the information behind that financial data.

- Does the data demonstrate a trend?
- Is it a symptom of something right or something wrong?
- Does it indicate how a particular situation can be improved?
- Are there suggestions for alternatives or innovative improvements?

It is necessary to remember that financial data is historical so the Finance crew is also required to look to consider the potential future. This means going beyond mere "number crunching" and emphasizing value-add in the Finance function of the ship.

Sam knows that to be a good captain she needs to be sensible when it comes to the allocation and use of funds as the ship's fuel. Borrowing money may be necessary for a certain project, but mismanaged debt can be like a hole in the hull – it can sink the ship. A sensible and responsible captain and Finance team will keep close tabs on costs and pay attention to dashboard indicators and gauges to keep debt levels under control.

Staying the Course

Sam keeps a close eye on her ship's dashboard at Bright Beacon Ltd. and uses the following indicators to monitor the fuel:

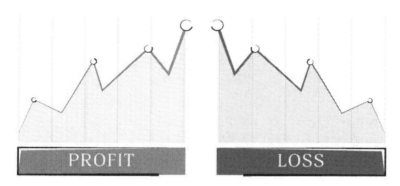

Profit & Loss Statement (P&L) - enables the captain to assess the past performance of the organization. This financial statement provides a summary of the revenues, costs, expenses, and profits of an organization for a specific period. The information in these records indicates whether an organization is able to generate a profit by increasing revenue, reducing costs and expenses, or a combination of both. A simplified P&L statement can be seen below, along with the FOAMSHIP officers who are primarily responsible for each component.

P&L Components	Officer in Charge
Revenues (fuel source from customers)	Marketing
- Costs of Goods/Services (fuel used in production)	Operations
= Gross Profit	Operations
- Expenses (fuel used in administration)	Finance
= Net Profit (fuel into reserves)	Captain

Sam can use the data found in this statement to analyze Bright Beacon Ltd.'s overall profitability and long-term sustainability. The dashboard's P&L gauge shows the captain how well the ship has produced fuel in the past.

~ FOAMSHIP ~
Shaping Organizational Success

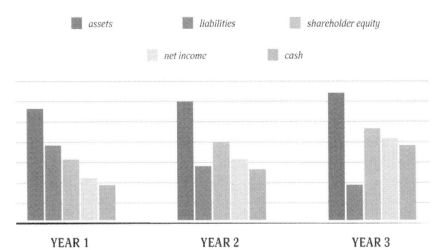

Balance Sheet (B/S) - enables the captain to assess the organization's current financial situation. It is a financial statement that reflects the organization's assets, liabilities, and equity at a single point in time. The data in this statement indicates what an organization owns, versus what it owes. Using the FOAMSHIP model will assist in ensuring that the ship's liabilities do not outweigh its assets. A simplified B/S statement is shown below, along with the FOAMSHIP Officers who are primarily responsible for each component.

B/S Components	Officer in Charge
Assets (the fuel we think we have)	Finance
- Liabilities (the fuel we will spend)	Finance
= Equity (the fuel we really have)	Captain

Sam uses these figures to calculate Bright Beacon Ltd.'s overall financial health and position for long-term stability. The B/S gauge displays the ship's fuel (cash) reserves for long-haul voyages.

~ FOAMSHIP ~
Shaping Organizational Success

CASH FLOW

E   F

Cash Flow Statement (CF) - enables the captain to forecast the future cash needs (fuel supply) required by the organization to stay afloat. The CF Statement provides a summary of the amount of money that is coming into and going out of, an organization. This measures how effectively the ship manages its fuel supply and if the fuel being pumped into the tanks is sufficient to keep the engines going. A simplified CF statement is represented below, along with the FOAMSHIP officers who are primarily responsible for each component.

CF Components	Officer in Charge
Cash In (the expected fuel inflows)	Finance
- Cash Out (the expected fuel outflows)	Finance
= Net Cash (to fuel reserves)	Captain

The CF statement is a tool Sam uses to determine Bright Beacon Ltd.'s ability to meet all of its financial obligations and responsibilities on time. The CF gauge indicates how much fuel the ship requires to reach its next destination, as well as the ports planned for future voyages. In the business world, the common phrase "cash is king" emphasizes the importance of a strong cash flow.

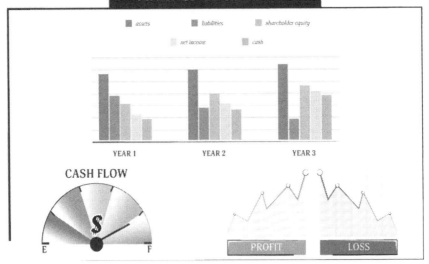

Implementing the FOAMSHIP model across the board within an organization will assist in gaining benefits that will be directly reflected in the financial statements.

All Hands on Deck

FOAMSHIP captains, officers, and shipmates also need to consider ways in which to keep the fuel supply streaming steadily into the ship's fuel tanks.

Invest in the customer experience

Customers replenish the fuel supply of an organization by buying its products or services. Whether a captain, officer, or shipmate, every soul on board the ship has an impact on how much fuel a customer will be willing to add. It is essential to pay attention to customer feedback; as well as to note what is not being mentioned.

~ FOAMSHIP ~
Shaping Organizational Success

Positive comments shine a light on an organization's strengths and negative comments reveal its weaknesses. Both aspects of customer opinion are important because it is easier to keep a current customer than it is to acquire a new one. Negative encounters such as poor service, inferior product quality, or unpleasant interactions cause tremendous harm to the ship in the form of reputational damage. Issues such as these must be addressed and rectified to improve the customer experience. Positive dealings will increase the organization's ability to retain existing customers and attract new ones.

Plan for the long haul, not just the next port of call

Financial planning enables the ability to meet strategic goals and achieve the captain's vision of where the ship is Heading. Without a clear plan in place, the crew can very easily lose sight of the ship's financial situation. Implementing cost control mechanisms is imperative to ensure that there are no fuel leaks along the way.

Although celebrating short-term successes is excellent for the morale of the crew, potential long-term consequences must not be overlooked. Sometimes, no amount of planning can prevent the ship from sailing into a perfect storm, but forethought and preparation will assist in weathering it until the sun breaks through the clouds once more.

Do things right the first time

Doing things "half-baked" can be costly. Investing in the best possible equipment, systems, and resources the ship can afford is beneficial to a smart long-term strategy. Funds should be allocated wisely to ensure a good balance between cost-effectiveness and quality. Cheap can often end up being more expensive in the long run so initiatives should be funded properly.

The ship's crew needs reliable tools to perform their duties and the impact this can have on products and services cannot be emphasized enough. Everything from computers to operational systems to the materials used in manufacturing affects the end product or service. Customers will make a decision about an organization based on what they receive – both in terms

of the deliverable and the experience. Remember, there's never a second chance to make a first impression.

Compensate and reward talent

Quality has a price, and so do good people. During lean times, companies sometimes make the mistake of reducing salaries as a cost-cutting measure. When the upturn comes, the crew then upgrades to a more rewarding company because their loyalty was lost. It costs more to replace good employees than to keep them happy; and the same is true for customers.

Sam and Fran know that they must keep an ear to the ground and feel the pulse of the crew. Not only do unhappy shipmates bring down the morale of their fellow crew members, but they can also have a negative impact on customers. In her role as a leader, Sam takes the advice of an undeniably successful captain, Richard Branson. His strong views on how to treat crew members echo her own and Sam agrees that "if you take care of your employees, they will take care of the clients". She also wants to be the type of captain who promotes a happy and healthy working environment. To this end, she strives to encourage, support, and value every member of her crew.

> *"I have always believed that the way you treat your*
> *employees is the way they will treat your customers, and*
> *that people flourish when they are praised."*
> *Richard Branson*

Taking care of her crew members is not only the right thing to do, as Sam believes, but it also has the subsequent benefit of enhancing the customer experience. Happy crew members lead to happy customers, and happy customers add more fuel to the ship.

Finance needs to provide feedback and involve everyone

Measurements and metrics provide feedback on the ship's present position and whether the current voyage is proving to be successful. It's good practice to periodically report on the "state of the ship" to all crew members.

~ FOAMSHIP ~
Shaping Organizational Success

Many organizations adopt an "open book" policy regarding the company's finances. Openly sharing this information with employees establishes and feeds the trust of the collective soul. Creating a work environment where everyone is aware of the financial position motivates the crew to pay close attention to details and performance measures. In doing so, their focused approach can positively impact the bottom lines.

Another approach to financial involvement is profit sharing. When compensation is tied to the bottom line, people naturally treat the organization's money as their own. Individuals start considering how their actions impact the bottom line and this can change their perspective in many positive ways.

Regardless of which structure and approach are adopted by an organization, consideration of the costs involved in every activity will help the ship reach its destination. Even the smallest fuel-conservation efforts, such as turning off lights in areas not in use or using resources sparingly, can make a difference to the overall success of a voyage.

In summary,

The Finance function should be the partner-in-charge for assessing value-creating opportunities in all areas of the organization.

Fran realizes that he can apply the same principles and approaches to his personal life, as well as in his role as an officer aboard the Bright Beacon Ltd. FOAMSHIP. Thoroughly analyzing the different alternatives and weighing costs versus benefits helps Fran to devise his own financial strategy. Conserving cash and allocating fuel reserves wisely, enables him to undertake the voyages that are most beneficial to achieving his personal life goals.

In both the business and personal contexts, financial resources provide the fuel to power the ship along its course. Without sufficient fuel supply, the ship will not reach its destination and the business objectives will not be achieved. Strong financial management is crucial to the success of any organization.

Examples: Finance

Consult the FOAMSHIP online case library (www.foamship.com/cases) to learn from extraordinary captains and hone your own captain skills. These exemplary companies offer valuable real-life examples of how to effectively work the Finance function.

Key Points: Finance

Review the key discussion points for this chapter.

FINANCE

The ship's fuel tanks, where we:

- Provide value-added insight and analysis on the financial well-being of the ship.
- Ensure there is sufficient cash for those short trips and long voyages.
- Compensate and reward talented crew properly so they won't jump ship.
- Constantly look for ways to conserve fuel and protect our fuel supply (customers).

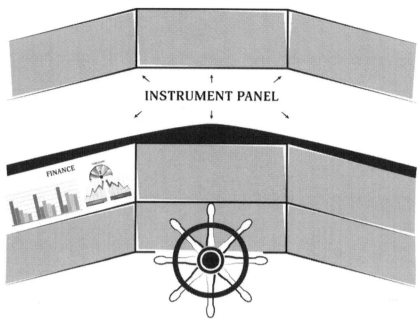

Remember to keep a close eye on your instrument panel to monitor the gauges of each FOAMSHIP component's dashboard.

Pulpit: Finance

Use these questions to hone your skills in applying the FOAMSHIP model in practice.

1. Consider ways in which your organization can reduce costs. Such as material purchases, equipment repairs, workflow, etc.
2. Are you and your fellow crew members aware of your organization's financial standing? If not, what can be done to rectify this?
3. Think of any potential alliances or partnerships that would help your organization leverage its resources and increase revenues and profits.
4. Do you think that some of the Finance guidelines presented in this chapter can be applied to your personal finances? If so, consider which ones and how you would apply them.

~ FOAMSHIP ~
Shaping Organizational Success

4. OPERATIONS: CREATING PRODUCTS AND SERVICES

"Excellence, then, is not an act, but a habit."

Aristotle

For a ship to travel full-steam ahead, it needs to convert fuel into thrust. The term "Operations" may bring to mind images and sounds of machinery and other inanimate objects found within factories and manufacturing plants. In reality, Operations are the people, equipment, and processes that generate business activity within an organization; whether it manufactures turbines or provides cleaning services.

As with any mechanical device, it is necessary to regularly fine-tune the operational component of an organization or it will become inefficient. Equally important is providing training and continuous education to the people who operate the equipment and tools so that their skills and abilities are also fine-tuned.

Operations can be extremely complex nowadays due to the level of sophistication and advances in technology, manufacturing, logistics, research and development, distribution, and the geographic spread of operations e.g., outsourcing. Although the purpose of this chapter is not to delve deeply into specific topics such as Production Planning and Control or Computer Integrated Manufacturing, it will demonstrate how everything fits together within the FOAMSHIP model. The Operations component of each organization is unique, but if it operates more efficiently than its competitors, it'll lead the race.

To reach lucrative customer ports, crew members in Operations must build products or deliver services that fulfill the customers' needs; and do so in the most competitive way possible.

29

There are many tools available that can be utilized to fine-tune a ship's engines. Popular methodologies such as LEAN Six Sigma and Balanced Scorecard are just two examples. These can be used to improve overall organizational performance by eliminating waste in processes and procedures.

Process Diagrams/Flowcharts

A very useful field tool to fine-tune a ship's engines is the process diagram, also known as a flowchart. Although process diagrams can be time-consuming to develop, the insight gained from the exercise can be beneficially revealing. This tool is not only applicable to the Operations business area, but can also be applied to the other functional FOAMSHIP areas of Finance, Administration, and Marketing.

In its most basic form, a process diagram illustrates the steps necessary to accomplish a specific task. As an example, a boat manufacturer can be considered here, and the task of painting the hull. In reality, this would be a complex process, but it can be simplified here to 3 basic steps as illustrated below:

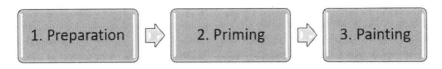

Each of these steps would then also include sub-steps in terms of 3 main inputs – the labor, materials, and equipment required to perform each step of the hull painting process. Additionally, it would also be necessary to determine the time required to perform each step because, if you can't measure it, you can't improve it. Although this is a very simplified example, when time is taken to document processes in all areas of a real-world organization, opportunities for improvement are almost guaranteed to be found. Processes also evolve over time, so periodic fine-tuning can be a powerful organizational habit.

Value Chain

Just as Marketing's message bonds with customers (discussed in a later chapter), Operations' message must establish a strong communication channel with suppliers. In doing so, Operations become part of the value chain that links demand with supply. It's the flow through the value-chain that will ultimately determine how well an organization can compete in the marketplace. The goal is to keep the work throughput flowing as smoothly

and seamlessly as possible by removing obstacles and bottlenecks, whether physical or metaphorical. An organization should strive for ship-shape equipment and a ship-shape mentality. This will elevate crew members into the "zone" where productivity soars to a notably higher level.

Sam regularly meets with Fran and the crew to discuss ways in which everyone can contribute to a smooth-running engine at Bright Beacon Ltd.

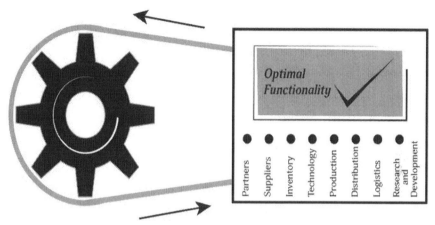

Adding Value to Operations

When considering ways to add value to Operations, it's helpful to picture contributors to the value-chain as parts of the ship's engine, which is illustrated above. From the Research and Development crew creating new products to those delivering the products physically or via a web portal, all departments use technology to reduce costs and provide added value to the customer. This in turn thrusts the organizational ship forward. Like an engine, all parts must operate in sequence and synchronicity for the machinery to operate effectively.

One of Sam's responsibilities as captain is to identify suppliers, resources, and improvements that will add the most value to each product or service that is being delivered by her organization, Bright Beacon Ltd.
She needs to ask and answer questions such as:

- Does sourcing from a low-wage country make greater economic sense than buying from a local supplier?
- Should suppliers be brought "on board" to become part of the value delivery process?

- Are LEAN and Just-in-Time methods being implemented to optimize all processes?
- Can web and mobile technologies be better used to expedite orders and payments?
- Are physical premises truly required, or would a virtual office be more feasible and beneficial?

Sam trusts her crew to be the best at what they do, so she also seeks their perspective and input when considering these questions. Involvement from Fran and the shipmates of all relevant departments ensures that Sam has the information and insight she needs to explore options, reach the best answers, and implement innovative and effective solutions.

Staying the Course

Aboard a ship, a combination of fuel and air is fed into the engine, goes through a chemical-mechanical conversion process, and generates thrust to propel the ship forward. A similar process exists within any business.

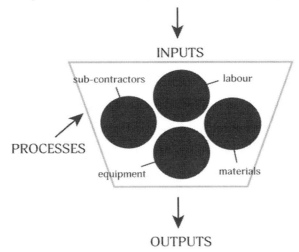

The four main inputs are:
- Labor
- Materials
- Equipment, and
- Subcontractors

These four inputs are processed to create a product or service, or a combination of both. The product or service is then delivered to the end-

~ FOAMSHIP ~
Shaping Organizational Success

user, or customer. The dashboards that make up the ship's instrument panel enable the captain to monitor all aspects of this process. Sam understands that to build an effective instrument panel for Bright Beacon Ltd., the gauges or dials of the ship's dashboards must reflect items that are quantifiable – if it cannot be measured, it cannot be improved. Each organization has its own unique needs, so it is Sam's responsibility to determine what must be measured to keep Bright Beacon Ltd. on course.

Inputs: Any business needs to optimize its use of labor, materials, equipment, and subcontractors to produce its product or service as efficiently as possible. Therefore, the dashboard dial measures the costs of these inputs and will be specific to each particular organization. The cheapest option is not always the best, however, so it's crucial to consider the balance between cost and quality.

Example 1: A boat manufacturer needs to keep track of costs related to the labor hours, all parts, and any equipment required to build one boat.

Example 2: A residential construction company requires its Operations dashboard to track the daily labor, materials, and equipment costs associated with building each house.

Example 3: A fast-food operation will strive to keep tight control of its labor and material supplies in order to remain competitive in the market.

Example 4: An IT company requires gauges to track investments in technology, as well as talent and emerging software and hardware.

Incorporating the relevant and applicable gauges on its Operations dashboard will assist each type of company to maximize its productivity.

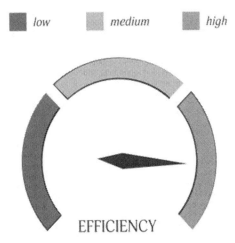

Processes: The success of any business is determined by how efficiently it converts its 'inputs' into 'outputs' in the form of beneficial products and services. There are many ways of measuring this efficiency within the ship's engine room, and each will depend on the specific type of business.

Example 1: The boat manufacturer will require its gauges to monitor Job Costs, Production Pipeline, and the number of boats that can be produced per week.

Example 2: The residential construction company's dashboard will need to measure Work-in-Progress, Completion Percentage, and the number of houses that can be built per month.

Example 3: The fast-food operation needs gauges that will assist in monitoring and minimizing the wastage of materials, and keeping tight control of daily Food & Labor costs.

Example 4: The IT company will benefit from an Operations dashboard that enables it to monitor and track Product Development Cycles to maintain sustainability.

CUSTOMER SATISFACTION

Outputs: To be successful, organizations must strive to deliver high levels of customer satisfaction, with the goal of meeting or exceeding expectations. The dashboard gauges and dials must be designed to capture this critical information in a way that is relevant and useful to the specific business.

Organizations can monitor customer satisfaction levels through various avenues such as traditional surveys, social media interactions, or the number of sales per customer. Unhappy customers typically express their discontent via survey tools, negative social media reviews, and buying fewer products.

It's important for the boat manufacturer, the construction company, the fast-food operation, and the IT company to ensure that their dashboards are designed in a way that best measures customer satisfaction levels for their specific business.

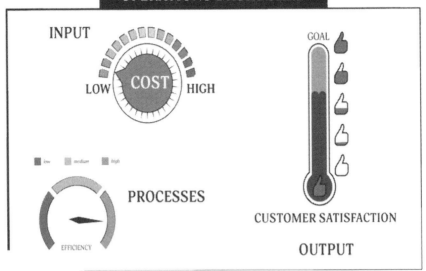

The FOAMSHIP model illustrates how the operational inputs and outputs are tied to other organizational components. As described in chapter 3, Finance: Generating Cash for Fuel, one of the purposes of the Profit & Loss Statement is to capture costs related to labor, material, equipment, and subcontractors – the operational inputs. The officer in charge of Operations is directly responsible and accountable for monitoring and controlling these variables to ensure that the engine room operates as smoothly as possible.

The operational outputs are also tied to the Marketing component, which will be discussed in chapter 6. Even after the product or service has been delivered, Customer Service must continue to maintain healthy and positive customer relationships. The officer in charge of Marketing is, therefore, responsible for maintaining superior Customer Service levels and distinguishing the ship from its competitors.

<u>All Hands on Deck</u>

In order for a ship to operate optimally and be "firing on all cylinders", the following elements must be incorporated:

Use technology to gain a competitive edge

The engine block of the ship can be thought of as the "corporate crankcase". It is here that the explosive energy of the pistons is converted into rotational power, and transferred to the propellers. Taking full advantage of technology when applying it to the engine will give an organization a significant competitive edge.

Train captains and crew in best practices

What proven methods or processes can be applied to this ship?

This is a question that every organization should ask regularly. Adopting approaches that have been shown to work well is a relatively reliable improvement as the guesswork has been taken out of the equation.

Operating crews must also be provided with proper and ongoing training to ensure that they remain current on the latest technologies and practices. Crews that are knowledgeable and skilled in areas such as supplier relationship management, seamless distribution systems, outstanding customer service delivery, and advanced business-to-business (B2B) tools result in an engine that purrs like a kitty cat.

Examine and evaluate regularly to meet business demands

Just as it is necessary for ships to regularly stop in at shipyards for repairs, overhauls, and maintenance, it is also essential for an organization to follow this example. Whether scraping the barnacles off of the hull, rebuilding the entire engine, or simply performing some light routine maintenance, it's imperative to always look for ways in which to improve Operations.

Everything should be questioned to determine whether there are better ways to fulfill each aspect of Operations. After all, in many cases, this is the number one way in which to improve the bottom line. This is particularly true for extremely competitive environments where the marketplace establishes that an organization can only charge so much for its particular product or service.

Leverage resources

There are numerous innovative ways in which to leverage resources to improve Operations. Seek help from business partners and utilize their strengths to combat weaknesses. Listen carefully to feedback from customers, suppliers, and employees to determine where improvements are needed and how these might be achieved.

A supplier may be willing to put a resident parts warehouse in your facility which could result in the drastic reduction of shipping costs. Perhaps a competitor can become a partner in a joint venture which would benefit both organizations. Airline alliances are a perfect example of this concept. A crew member might have a suggestion on how to streamline a process that would conserve resources and increase output. Innovative ideas can come from multiple sources and Operations can always be improved.

Innovate, differentiate, or evaporate

Even if the organization does not have a dedicated Research and Development department, captains and crews should always be on the look-out for new ways of delivering products and services. Continuous improvement is essential in all areas of the ship – from people and processes to products or services.

Always bear in mind that no matter what an organization does, there is always room for improvement. Successful organizations embrace innovation and strive to differentiate themselves from the competition in order to provide better for their customers.

~ FOAMSHIP ~
Shaping Organizational Success

Examples: Operations

Consult the FOAMSHIP online case library (www.foamship.com/cases) to learn from extraordinary captains and hone your own captain skills. These exemplary companies offer valuable real-life examples of how to effectively improve Operations.

Key Points: Operations

Review the key discussion points for this chapter.

OPERATIONS

The engine room of our ship where we:

- Create the products and services which propel our ship forward.
- Use technology to build solid links with suppliers and provide added value to customers.
- Keep the crew ship-shape by providing the latest training in best practices.
- Continuously fine-tune the engine to provide efficient product and service delivery.
- Constantly monitor processes to identify improvement opportunities.

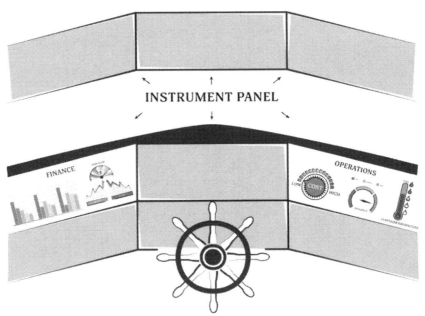

Remember to keep a close eye on your instrument panel to monitor the gauges of each FOAMSHIP component's dashboard.

Pulpit: Operations

Use these questions to hone your skills in applying the FOAMSHIP model in practice.

1. Consider ways in which you can improve the Operations of your particular work area or circle of influence. Then do the same for your entire organization as a whole.
2. Review some of your organization's supplier relationships. In what ways can the FOAMSHIP model assist in making these relationships stronger?
3. Brainstorm ways in which you and your organization can become more innovative and more competitive.
4. What steps can you take to elevate your level of personal productivity?

40

5. ADMINISTRATION: LEADING FROM THE HELM

"Great companies need both a visionary entrepreneur and a skilled executive: one for the top line, the other for the bottom line"

Howard Schultz (Former CEO, Starbucks Coffee)

Aboard the FOAMSHIP, Administration refers to managing the most important asset on board – the people. In this context, Administration is akin to the Human Resources (HR) Department within a traditional organization. The FOAMSHIP model aims to create the best captains, officers, and shipmates by maximizing the potential of each individual.

The management team consists of the captain and officers, each with particular skill sets and critical roles. The competency of the captain and officers in steering the ship will determine how far it can travel and what destinations can be reached. A strong and well-balanced management team will benefit from captains with entrepreneurial traits, and officers with intrapreneurial skills.

Essential Skills

People have different skills and abilities, and there are many kinds of testing tools available to determine an individual's entrepreneurial or managerial aptitudes, or whether they're a combination of both (intrapreneur). Numerous factors influence working potential, and these include:

- Cultural background
- Upbringing
- Social variables
- Education levels
- Personal beliefs

In trying to determine what makes good business captains and officers, it's helpful to consider the character profiles of both entrepreneurs and managers.

According to research into the subject, a typical entrepreneur:

- Is intuitive in perceiving customers' unmet needs
- Seizes high-quality opportunities
- Possesses a strong internal drive to see a venture through
- Is open to new experiences and eager to learn new ways to solve problems
- Is able to deal with ambiguity
- Is flexible and actively responsive to change
- Accepts failure and is not defeated by it
- Is motivated by opportunity and independence
- Is innovative and creative
- Focuses on the long-term goal as well as what is needed to achieve it
- Trusts instincts to overcome obstacles ✦
- Is willing to assume higher levels of risk

~ FOAMSHIP ~
Shaping Organizational Success

While a business manager is generally more prone to:

- Be concerned with proper resource allocation
- Be adept at organizing and motivating people
- Handling the coordination of tasks
- Supervising, influencing, and leading people
- Delegating effectively
- Be comfortable with steady environments
- Keeping the organization running smoothly
- Inward orientation regarding their own practices
- Perception of immediate events within their control
- Adhere to structure and the status quo
- Avoid mistakes
- Focusing on short-term goals
- Being motivated by standard rewards like power and promotion

Entrepreneurs usually tend to have a risk-taking type of personality and this serves them well as it enables them to follow their dreams and vision. Following this path requires them to take an idea and run with it. Due to this, it is often the case that they have to adopt a "jack of all trades, master of none" approach to bring their ideas to fruition.

43

 ~ FOAMSHIP ~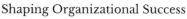
Shaping Organizational Success

Managers, on the other hand, typically work in a well-defined environment, with a steady and predictable paycheck, and different pressures to those experienced by the entrepreneur. A manager's area of control is smaller and their risks are, for the most part, borne by their organization.

Although these types of individuals differ greatly, they each have strengths that can be enhanced, and weaknesses which can be improved upon. Sam knows that a true business captain is always learning and gaining new skills and knowledge. To fulfill her role and responsibilities in an exceptional manner, Sam must not only work on her own abilities but also encourage her crew to do the same. Fran is one of an emerging breed known as "entrepreneurial managers" or "intrapreneurs" and Sam supports him in exploring this mindset. She believes that promoting Fran's innovative approach will greatly benefit Bright Beacon Ltd., while also helping him to grow both personally and professionally.

Teamwork

Any organization needs a crew with different character profiles to achieve success. Some business activities require entrepreneurial instincts, while others demand command-and-control attributes. It's essential to understand this division of duties because when one person tries to do everything alone, it can have a less than desirable outcome. For an organization to truly thrive, it's important to also understand the need for multiple skill sets. A successful approach requires tactical and technical skills, and it's very challenging for one person to effectively deliver both. While a captain is thinking strategically and tactically, a strong crew is needed to sell the product or service, produce or deliver it, and manage the cash flow.

As a good captain, Sam recognizes that she must surround herself with officers who complement her strengths and compensate for her weaknesses. Captains and officers, such as Sam and Fran, working in tandem are best suited to resolve multiple issues and cover all the bases. Sam also understands that allowing officers like Fran to manage the ship gives her more space and energy to focus on guiding it towards her vision.

Management Styles

There are a vast number of management styles that can be practiced and the adopted style will have a significant impact on the culture within the organization. A very outdated approach to management is ruling by fear and intimidation. This leads to a culture where crew members live in a constant state of anxiety and dread. A negative environment such as this breeds distress, panic, and apprehension – which are all forces that stunt the development of crew members. When people work in a toxic setting, they are far less likely to propose innovative ideas, be their most productive selves, or foster a sense of loyalty to their ship and captain.

Sam and Fran agree that a more positive and beneficial management style is one that focuses on motivation rather than fear. Crew members are encouraged to take responsibility for their actions and the consequences and to be accountable for their performance and the results. At Bright Beacon Ltd. a culture of effective self-management is promoted. This creates a work environment that can efficiently handle all business operations, from productivity to adversity. A healthy atmosphere onboard the ship will nurture independent thinking, problem-solving, and conflict management. Organizations that reward teamwork, share success and endorse overall well-being will be more prosperous in their endeavors.

Delegating

It's a part of human nature to resist change. This means that it can be challenging for people to accept new responsibilities that make them accountable. Many things can make people hesitant to embrace responsibility, such as previous roles where the consequences were severe if the desired results were not attained. A frequently seen phenomenon is people's fear or unwillingness to make decisions, even simple ones. This situation results in the crew taking all decisions to the captain to avoid making them for themselves. When this is a prevalent scenario within an organization, it can also be a sign that the captain is not delegating effectively. When decisions are not made at the appropriate levels, it can create a bottleneck which is a significant growth inhibitor.

When an organizational culture develops that dictates every decision must flow to the top, the only true growth will be that of the captain's mental capacity and abilities. This would also then lead to the captain being required on the bridge 24 hours a day, which is neither a healthy nor a beneficial expectation.

To maintain a positive balance, Sam knows that one of her key objectives as captain is to empower her crew to make decisions on their own, with confidence. Experience is a factor in good decision-making, but clear directives on the desired outcomes also play a significant role. Trusting and believing in Fran and the rest of her crew enables Sam to focus on her own roles and responsibilities in guiding her ship.

Continued Improvement

A strong captain constantly challenges themselves and their crew to be the best they can be. It's necessary to benchmark an organization against other business vessels as a way of looking for areas of improvement.

Using the FOAMSHIP model as a method of introspection can reveal that crew members might be duplicating efforts, focusing on trivial matters, or performing tasks without the required training. Common work areas for informal dialogue and idea exchange are an excellent way to share information amongst the crew and create organizational knowledge.

Communication is Key

The importance of communication should never be underestimated in any area of life, on professional and personal levels. It is the very foundation of effective and efficient change management, and leadership as a whole. Strong communication channels within an organization are absolutely vital to its success.

Just as a ship cannot safely and successfully navigate its passage and stay on course without clear instruction, neither can an organization achieve its goals without effective communication, trust, and transparency. It's crucial for Sam to be a willing communicator and to use her leadership skills to affect change across the entire ship. She must be able to effectively manage the fear of change, volatility, uncertainty, complexity, and ambiguity within her organization. Not "losing her cool" under pressure is also imperative because her crew needs her the most during times of turbulent seas.

FOAMSHIP directs captains, officers, and shipmates into their respective roles and responsibilities to more effectively steer the organizational vessel.

All Hands on Deck

The FOAMSHIP model is not only beneficial at the larger organizational level but can also be applied to individual departments or divisions within a business. For example, the FOAMSHIP components can be considered in the context of the Human Resources Department's role in Administration.

Finance – the HR manager has P&L responsibility, especially in managing headcount and, therefore, must carefully manage the budget and fuel consumption for that department.

Operations – procedures need to be in place for talent searches, interviews, selection, training, and disciplinary actions.

Administration – a strong HR crew will include individuals who are skilled in areas such as compensation, and Labor Law.

Marketing – HR needs to have satisfied internal customers, namely the crew it serves, and a good reputation inside and outside the entity, so that people return when in need of its services.

Souls – the HR department's own crew members need to be motivated to perform as a team and to bring out the best of all the souls on board.

Heading – HR must have its goals clearly defined in order to preserve the ship's most valuable asset – its people.

~ FOAMSHIP ~
Shaping Organizational Success

Innovation – it's critical to encourage innovative thinking, employee development, and the sharing of information, from vision to performance results, to improve all areas of the ship.

Passage – HR must stay abreast of the job market to attract the best talent and set policies that will assist in effective navigation and keeping the ship on course.

Staying the Course

At the helm, Sam uses her ship's sophisticated and dynamic instrument panel to keep Bright Beacon Ltd. on course. The Finance dashboard indicates healthy fuel levels, the gauges of the Operations dashboard signify that production levels are optimal, and sales are being tracked by the Marketing dashboard.

Now Sam needs to build an Administration dashboard that integrates the human element, or Soul, into the other FOAMSHIP components. Quantifying this can be challenging, but various organizational elements can aid the measurements.

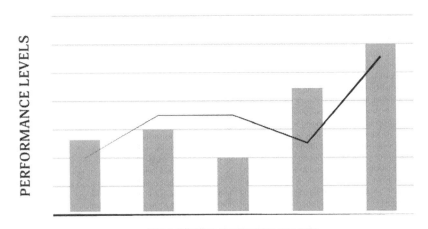

~ FOAMSHIP ~
Shaping Organizational Success

Training: An important metric to keep track of aboard our ship is Training. Investing in employee training sends a strong signal that a company is interested in developing its employees to their full potential.

Sam finds another quote from Richard Branson coming to mind when she checks her Training charts:

> *"Train people well enough so they can leave, treat them well enough so they don't want to."*

Good captains have a responsibility to help their crew develop and grow. Training creates a well-equipped crew and shows the crew members that their personal development is important to their organization. Taking care of the souls on board will also have the benefit of enhancing the ship's operations because happy crew members are productive crew members.

Fuel consumed by training costs is wasted when crew members abandon ship so it's important to retain them by treating them well. Developing and rewarding talent creates a mutualistic relationship between the ship and its crew where each one benefits from working together.

TURNOVER TRIGGERS

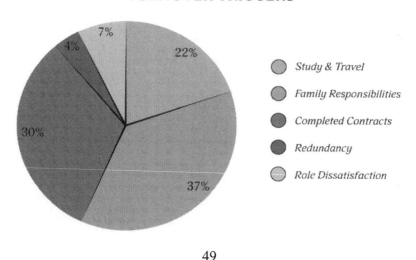

~ FOAMSHIP ~
Shaping Organizational Success

Turnover: Another essential metric to closely monitor is Employee Turnover. Many companies have a "revolving door" attitude towards crew members and this is a clear indication of the internal workings of an organization. The rate of employee turnover vs. employee retention is a direct reflection of its Soul. It cannot be emphasized enough that taking care of the crew is beneficial to the ship as a whole. When crew members are unhappy or dissatisfied, many elements are affected, such as:

- Overall morale
- Employee motivation
- Productivity
- Product/service quality
- Customer interaction
- Accuracy
- Organizational loyalty

High levels of employee turnover and low levels of retention are a warning siren that the ship has veered off course in terms of its crew. The Soul component of the FOAMSHIP model will discuss how a seasoned crew is more valuable to an organization than an ever-changing line-up of temporary shipmates. Sam and Fran both monitor the retention and turnover rates to ensure that Bright Beacon Ltd. doesn't lose any crew members overboard.

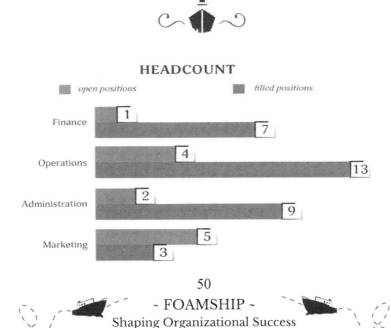

HEADCOUNT

open positions   filled positions

Department	open positions	filled positions
Finance	1	7
Operations	4	13
Administration	2	9
Marketing	5	3

~ FOAMSHIP ~
Shaping Organizational Success

Headcount: This is relatively straightforward and the data can easily be provided by the HR department. However, the more important aspect here is to measure and track the headcount against another variable, such as Cost of Goods Sold (COGS) or Cost of Sales (COS).

An example would be tracking the number of shipmates in the production department against the COGS or COS. This ratio would then provide a baseline measurement for when the ship is firing on all cylinders. If the number then trends upwards, there may be too many crew members in the engine room and restructuring may be necessary.

Similarly, tracking the total number of crew members in the home office against the total number within the organization can also yield useful information. An upward trend here can indicate that the overhead expenses are too high and that may also require restructuring efforts.

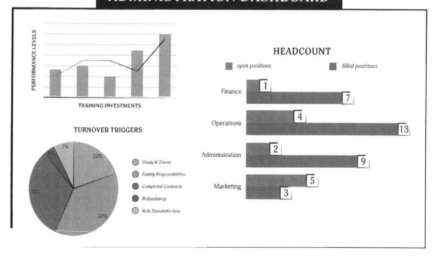

Examples: Administration

Consult the FOAMSHIP online case library (www.foamship.com/cases) to learn from extraordinary captains and hone your own captain skills. These exemplary companies offer valuable real-life examples of how to effectively implement strong and positive Administration.

Key Points: Administration

Review the key discussion points for this chapter.

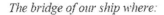

ADMINISTRATION

The bridge of our ship where:

- Our organization benefits from managerial, entrepreneurial, and intrapreneurial character profiles.
- Captains and officers complement each other's strengths and compensate for each other's weaknesses.
- The entire crew works together to maximize our ship's range.
- Captains and officers manage all the interdependencies of the FOAMSHIP components, to maintain the ship's course.
- Directives are clearly defined so everyone knows their roles and responsibilities.
- The approach to management fosters a healthy, supportive, and positive environment.

~ FOAMSHIP ~
Shaping Organizational Success

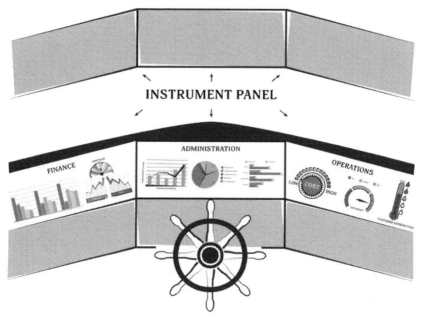

Remember to keep a close eye on your instrument panel to monitor the gauges of each FOAMSHIP component's dashboard.

Pulpit: Administration

Use these questions to hone your skills in applying the FOAMSHIP model in practice.

1. Would you consider your team, department, and organization to be well-managed? Why, or why not?
2. Review the entrepreneurial and managerial traits discussed in this chapter, and consider whether they are present or absent within your organization. Also, consider how many of these traits apply to you personally.
3. Brainstorm ways in which the qualities discussed in this chapter might be stimulated within yourself and all souls within your organization.
4. How can you apply some of these qualities to your personal voyage through life?

~ FOAMSHIP ~
Shaping Organizational Success

6. MARKETING: SELECTING CUSTOMER PORTS

"Business has only two functions – marketing and innovation."

Milan Kundera, Czech Writer

There are many organizational ships sailing across the business ocean. An organization's customers, suppliers, and competitors all navigate their own ships and have their own goals to achieve. Some of these other ships are allies, some are enemies. Marketing is a tool used to guide a ship to the right destination by identifying the best business opportunities. Today's rapidly changing marketplace requires an organization to have a very accurate guidance system to prevent the ship from getting lost, arriving at the wrong port, or not arriving at all.

The role of the Marketing function is to proactively identify customers and translate their wants and needs into desirable products and services, at the right time, place, and price.

The marketing battlefield has changed dramatically due to the continuous advancements in modern technology. Marketing is everywhere these days and it can't be escaped, avoided, or ignored. The evolving changes in demographics is also of key significance to the crew members in the marketing department. It is no longer sufficient to implement a "shotgun" strategy with the aim of being everything to everybody. International endeavors are even more complicated because different cultures perceive products and services in completely different ways. This makes it very challenging to conquer many oceans at once and it takes a seasoned captain and crew to cross international waters successfully.

The way in which customers perceive an organization will determine the ship's overall success in the long run. Some organizations focus so strictly on being business-driven that the result is a feeling of arrogance and

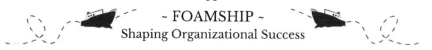

indifference. It's important to rather cultivate an atmosphere of trust, sincerity, and professionalism, as this is more likely to resonate positively in the minds of the customers.

This requires input and feedback directly from the organization's current and potential customers. Technology has made it possible for conversations with customers to happen in a seemingly endless number of ways and these can be used to gain valuable insight into customer opinion. An organization needs to know what its customers think of when using its product or service. It needs to gauge the value perceived by its customers when they think of the company's brand. Getting into the mind of the target audience is absolutely essential and this is a vital element of the marketing role.

As the ship navigates the passage to its destination port, the crew needs to convince the customers waiting at that port to truly believe that its product or service is the best choice. It's also necessary to ensure that the customers know that they can trust the captain and crew to provide consistently good service. Not only will this create a loyal customer base and positively position the product in the customers' minds, but it will also help customers to feel more comfortable. When a customer feels comfortable, they will provide feedback on how the products and services delivered by the ship are meeting, or not meeting, their needs and expectations. This, in turn, gives the organization insight that drives innovation and leads to new and improved products and services. In the current times, products and services typically co-exist as a bundle that together must provide value to the customer.

Catering directly to the wants and needs of the target customer can also minimize the amount of competition an organization must face. When implementing the FOAMSHIP model, it can be highly beneficial to integrate the concept developed by W. Chan Kim and Renée Mauborgne in their book entitled *"Blue Ocean Strategy"*. The tagline *"How to Create Uncontested Market Space and Make the Competition Irrelevant"* clearly outlines the marketing theory detailed in the book.

Simply put, the concept proposed by Kim and Mauborgne is for organizations to carve out their own new niche markets (blue oceans) to avoid doing battle in overly competitive existing markets (red oceans). This is done by clearly understanding the needs of the organization's customers, and drafting detailed navigational plans to deliver the promised goods with superior value and exceptional service.

~ FOAMSHIP ~
Shaping Organizational Success

Social Media and Public Relations

The impact of social media on marketing has been tremendous. In many ways, it has completely revolutionized the way organizations must approach marketing and public relations. Social networks provide a platform for instant interaction with individuals, customer groups, suppliers, and partners. Feedback relating to products and services can be seen by vast numbers of people instantaneously and simultaneously. This means that it is imperative to satisfy customers or run the risk of negative experiences being spread rapidly via word of mouth.

Additionally, the preference for mobile applications is on the rise and trends indicate that this will continue in the years to come. Mobile apps enable customers and suppliers to access information anywhere and at any time. The combination of social media and mobile apps makes it easy for people to connect with other consumers on an emotional and personal level, while buying and selling decisions can be made spontaneously.

The popularity of social networks and the abundance of mobile apps dedicated specifically to consumerism and its related feedback, makes it crucial for organizations to keep up with technological trends. If a business ship is to interact proactively with its customers, it must be equipped with the necessary tools. This is vital to the ship's success and if the captain and crew don't interact with customers effectively, the competition will. To identify the ship's level of efficiency in this area, there are questions that must be asked.

- Does the organization have "battle plans" that can lead it to success?
- Are there better channels to reach the target audience?
- Are the products and services being effectively managed in terms of branding, packaging, labelling, and positioning?
- Are the best strategies in place for marketing, advertising, publicity, public relations, sales, and promotions?

In a world of increasing interconnectedness, customers are constantly exposed to numerous value options and an endless array of choices. The marketing crew of any organizational ship is constantly faced with new challenges and opportunities triggered by people exchanging experiences instantly via Facebook, Instagram, Twitter, YouTube, and many other sites. This information, feedback, and insight must be used by the marketing function to capitalize on emerging opportunities that can make the ship the preferred choice of its customers.

Staying the Course

A wide array of metrics exists and choosing which to track and monitor is an important decision. Building the perfect dashboard is subjective and the gauges selected will depend on what the ship's captain needs to see. Each organizational vessel must customize its entire instrument panel to best suit its purpose and goals.

CUSTOMER SATISFACTION

Customer Satisfaction: There are many gauges that can assist in navigating an organizational ship across the oceans of industry, but Customer Satisfaction (CS) is generally considered to be the most important. A satisfied customer is likely to become a repeat customer who returns for more products and/or services. Returning customers continue to pump fuel into the ship's tanks. There are numerous ways to track and monitor Customer Satisfaction levels, such as:

- Traditional surveys
- Online surveys
- Social media channels
- Review boards
- Google Analytics
- Customer Relationship Management (CRM) systems

The data provided by these, and other, avenues will enable an organization to determine whether its customers are satisfied with its products and services, and act accordingly. The officer in charge of Marketing is responsible for measuring and monitoring this critical metric.

To improve the efforts of the marketing department, Fran requested that Sam invest some of Bright Beacon Ltd.'s cash fuel supply in a reliable CRM system. This software makes it possible to monitor, manage, and analyze all customer interactions. This not only includes current customers, but also past and potential customers. The valuable information collected by the CRM is beneficial across all departments of Bright Beacon Ltd. to assist in gaining new customers, and keeping existing ones.

CUSTOMER CONVERSION

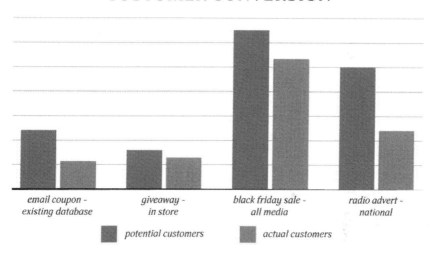

| email coupon - existing database | giveaway - in store | black friday sale - all media | radio advert - national |

■ potential customers   ■ actual customers

Customer Conversion Rate: There are a multitude of ways to acquire new business and the methods for doing so are as varied as the types of industries. Regardless of which approach to gaining new customers is adopted, it's essential to track the number of potential customers who are contacted, and measure how many of these are converted into actual customers.

The Actual Customers vs. Potential Customers metric is important because marketing can be a costly endeavor. Activities and items such as email campaigns, promotional merchandise, media advertising, etc. require a significant amount of resources. Therefore, the return on investment must be measurable to ensure that the fuel is not simply leaking from the tanks.

Determining which marketing activities are successful provides the information necessary to tailor further efforts to be effective.

SALES PER CUSTOMER

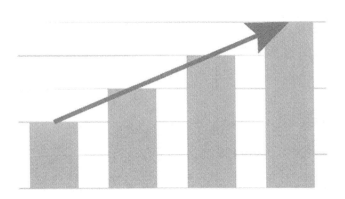

Sales per Customer: Once customers have boarded the ship, it's vital to track the number of products and/or services they consume. Obtaining the Sales per Customer (S/C) metric has been greatly simplified since the emergence of technology such as Point of Sales (POS) systems and online shopping carts. These automatically collect the data required for S/C analysis.

Using Google Analytics and other tools designed specifically for the analysis of customer databases can reveal additional insights into aspects such as customer buying habits and preferences. This is then used to increase the ratio of S/C by aligning marketing efforts and product/service offerings with the wants and needs of the target audience.

The tools used to collect this valuable marketing data are wide-ranging. Even the simplest of tools can provide the ability to convert this information into more sales. Whether the ship is a start-up getting ready for its maiden voyage or one of a large fleet preparing to launch yet another endeavor, there are relevant, beneficial, and easy-to-use tools available.

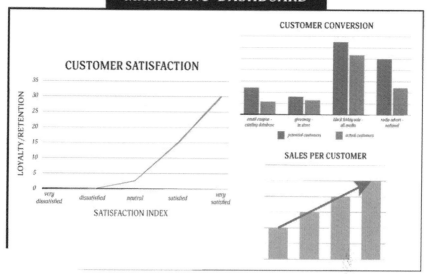

All Hands on Deck

Understand your business

It's surprising how many people work for companies that they don't understand. When asked what their organization does, the answers can be as vague as "Oh, we make some computer stuff" or "I guess we offer some kind of financial services". It appears that some people spend more time deciding what to wear to work, than they do understanding the place where they make their living.

Some organizations give brief introductory seminars to all new hires to provide them with a basic understanding of what the business offers in terms of products and services. It is advisable for companies to ensure a deeper

61

level of organizational knowledge amongst its crew members because every employee on the street is a potential salesperson – and a sale can materialize anywhere.

Be aware of your competition

Keeping an eye on the competition is not limited to business hours. Discovering new or improved products, services, processes, and procedures can happen anywhere, anytime. Whether at a formal networking event, on vacation in another country, or simply talking to an acquaintance, information and innovation can be found to enhance the ship's offerings. Pay attention to potential opportunities and what the competition is doing.

Invest in marketing intelligence

Having the best idea in the world, but no one to buy it, is like sending money to the bottom of the ocean faster than dropping anchor. Organizations need to be aware of what is available "out there", in terms of products and services that fulfill needs and bring satisfaction to customers.

This is a task that each and every crew member should incorporate into their responsibilities, not only those in the formal marketing roles. Many organizations reward their crews for good ideas that generate products, services, or cost-saving improvements. A ship's crew can provide an abundance of eyes and ears to scan the customer environment every day.

Allow innovation to bubble

Many products have been developed as a result of employee need or feedback. Most famous is probably the omnipresent yellow Post-It® Notes by 3M. A scientist was having trouble marking the pages of his hymnal at church and was frustrated enough by it to seek a solution. He subsequently created some "gooey-stuff" in his lab to fix paper notelets to the book's pages, and the Post-It® Note was born.

Similarly, Gillette has employees who volunteer to shave at work to offer insight and feedback on new products. This just proves that ideas can be generated anywhere – even in corporate bathrooms.

Differentiate yourself

It's important to identify what makes your organization better than the competition, and how to communicate the benefits of your products or services to your potential customers. In a world where many items are becoming commodities, it's necessary to find the leverage points with clients that make your offering superior in value.

For example, a product can be more expensive, yet still competitive, if the level of customer service is outstanding or the product quality is notably higher. Another example is when a brand is considered trendy or fashionable, such as coffee shops that charge higher prices because they offer a "cool and hip" environment.

To summarize, at the bow of a FOAMSHIP organization, the Marketing function acts like a radar, continuously scanning the horizon for emerging opportunities.

Examples: Marketing

Consult the FOAMSHIP online case library (www.foamship.com/cases) to learn from extraordinary captains and hone your own captain skills. These exemplary companies offer valuable real-life examples of how to effectively make the most of the Marketing function.

Key Points: Marketing

Review the key discussion points for this chapter.

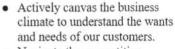

MARKETING

The compass of our ship which helps us to:

- Actively canvas the business climate to understand the wants and needs of our customers.
- Navigate the competitive battlefields to position our ship as the best choice.
- Guide our ship to relevant customer ports to provide the right products and/or services.
- Constantly create new and improved products and services to extend our ship's reach and range.
- Follow customer feedback to reach the highest levels of customer satisfaction.

~ FOAMSHIP ~
Shaping Organizational Success

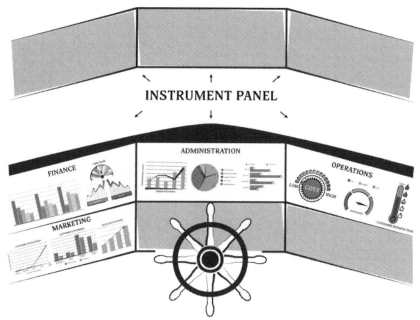

Remember to keep a close eye on your instrument panel to monitor the gauges of each FOAMSHIP component's dashboard.

Pulpit: Marketing

Use these questions to hone your skills in applying the FOAMSHIP model in practice.

1. Do you feel that your organization is meeting all the needs of its clients or customers? Why, or why not?
2. Do you have a good understanding of what constitutes a relevant "client port" for your organization? If not, what information would you require to clarify this?
3. Consider new products or services that could be offered to extend your organization's reach and range. Don't limit yourself to the current environment or constraints – i.e., "think outside the ship".
4. How could you better market yourself at work? In your community? In your life in general?

~ FOAMSHIP ~
Shaping Organizational Success

This concludes our coverage of the four traditional functional areas of business, namely:

- **F**inance
- **O**perations
- **A**dministration, and
- **M**arketing

Finance provides valuable insight and metrics on the voyage progress and fuel supply so that...
Operations can work efficiently to deliver products or services while...
Administration sets the course and coordinates teamwork to make things happen according to the strategy...
Marketing has devised after scanning the horizon for new and existing opportunities.

In the next chapter, we will cross over into the realm of the more "artistic" elements, to explore:

- **S**ouls
- **H**eading
- **I**nnovation, and
- **P**assage

Take a moment to review the first half of our journey to make sure that you're prepared for the next leg of the FOAMSHIP voyage!

7. SOULS ON BOARD

"Not everything that counts can be counted and not everything that can be counted, counts."

Albert Einstein

Bright Beacon Ltd. is running like a well-oiled machine and sailing full steam ahead towards its destination. Sam regularly reviews the progress her ship is making and checks all the gauges to make sure that everything remains on course. With her crew handling things smoothly, Sam takes some time to meet with Fran to discuss the future of Bright Beacon Ltd.

Together, Sam and Fran consider what they've discovered along their journey, so far:

- The significance of Finance in all organizations
- The essential need for Operations to be effective and efficient
- The importance of strong Administration at the helm of the business ship
- The benefits of up-to-date Marketing techniques and strategies

Both Sam and Fran believe in the products and services offered aboard their FOAMSHIP vessel, but they also know that there is always room for improvement. Although all the functional business components of the ship are being monitored and maintained, Sam feels like something is missing. She shares this feeling with Fran and they decide it is time to focus on the less tangible elements of the organization.

Together they considered some of the swashbucklers of the business world and business entities which could be seen as textbook-perfect in their operational aspects. There are many examples of such businesses which still failed because there was some intangible "thing" missing. An invisible force that brought together the collective energy of the crew members and used it for the benefit of all. The functional aspects of a business are vital, but over time, they alone are not enough to ensure a successful voyage.

~ FOAMSHIP ~
Shaping Organizational Success

Fran had previously worked in a similar middle management role for an organization that did not consider the human element. During his time with that company, he felt like every person was entirely on their own. There was an attitude of "Everybody fend for yourself!" and never mind the other souls on board.

The souls. It's the soul – the spirit, the *esprit de corps* – of an organization that can make the difference between success and failure. That was the missing "something" that Sam instinctively knew must be nurtured at Bright Beacon Ltd. Listening to Fran speak of how unhappy he'd been in his previous role made it abundantly clear to Sam that there is more to keeping a crew happy than just taking care of all things practical.

It's the soul of an organization that colors everything from the atmosphere to the attitude of everyone on board. Like a choir when each person singing is on the same page and in key, the sound is beautiful because it resonates with the collective soul. Humans require soul in their surroundings to truly flourish. This is the spark that ignites creativity, dedication, initiative, innovation, loyalty, and morale. The soul of an organization is what makes it a "bad" place to work, a "good" place to work, or a great place to work. At the heart of any organizational ship is the collective force, energy, or spirit of all the crew members and this is what defines it. Thus:

The Soul is composed of emotional, intellectual, and spiritual energies, which enables individuals to contribute not only rational and analytical capabilities but also an intuitive and creative genius.

Soul as an Organizational Concept

As abstract as the concept of Soul may sound, it's truly important in organizations with a desire to excel and succeed. Captains, in particular, need to understand and nurture the soul of their ship because it can make or break the vessel. The basic element of any organization is the unique and multi-faceted human being, and the collection of these individuals makes up an organizational "being". This "being" is as alive as the talents, values, virtues, faults, prejudices, energies, and attitudes that the collective crew brings to the organization.

Picturing the soul as precious cargo aboard the FOAMSHIP enables the ability to combine the intangible human aspects of an organization with the more tangible side of the business – bringing art to the science of management. Awakening or reinforcing the soul increases an organization's operational efficiency and productivity, while also boosting individual and collective morale. By bringing people together through the mutual understanding of a common frame of reference, FOAMSHIP elevates the positive energies of empowerment and success from the individual level to the collective group level.

Sam took some time to visit each department of Bright Beacon Ltd. so that she could learn more about the soul of her ship. To ensure objectivity, she asked Fran to do the same and report back to her with his findings. They both noticed that although the soul emanating from some departments was palpably positive, there were others where things didn't look nor feel right.

Marketing was led by a lively, exciting, and creative manager and his energy permeated the whole department, with the marketing shipmates echoing this attitude. Images of "whistling while you work" came to mind and the productivity level data supported the theory that a happy crew is a productive crew.

In stark contrast, the IT department had a "temple of doom" atmosphere, with a stern and overly-serious manager who kept his shipmates' noses to the grindstone. Despite being all work and no play, productivity remained below the desired level and this proved to Sam that morale has a direct impact on the efficiency of the crew.

Sam and Fran also noticed that the negative energy emanating from the IT department did not remain confined there. It flowed throughout the ship and afflicted other departments and shipmates. This showed them that soul energy, both positive and negative, can be present as "islands" within an organization, but that the net effect is that the bad tends to override the good.

Soul can be referred to as the "character of the culture" within an organization. It is the entire emotional and intellectual spectrum that brings the ship to life. The responsibility of the organization's leaders is to make the most of the power and talent available aboard the ship.

A vigorous soul, with high levels of positive energy, will create an environment with a great flow of ideas and innovation. This innovation brings success, which in turn, replenishes the soul with more energy in a powerful cycle that leads to bigger and better inventions. Therefore, it is the duty of true captains and officers to arouse, inspire, and harness the soul

energy. To build and strengthen the ship's soul, it's necessary to instill in the work environment as many positive leadership qualities as possible. The right attitude contributes to the creation of a high-energy atmosphere that translates into enthusiasm and encourages both the individual and the organization to strive for mutual success.

All Hands on Deck

During a brainstorming session, Sam and Fran consider the role of leadership in nurturing the soul of the ship. It stands to reason that if a leader strongly influences the soul of a department or organization, then that leader also significantly influences how the energy is driven forward. Together they determined which principles and desirable qualities would be most beneficial to encourage aboard the FOAMSHIP, and how these could be used to guide the actions of all those on board – from captains to officers to shipmates.

1. Attitude and Accountability

A positive attitude is an extremely powerful force. A person's ability to understand and control their emotions under different personal, social, and work-related situations is referred to as personal EQ (Emotional Quotient). Studies have shown that personal EQ is just as important as IQ (Intelligence Quotient) in determining an individual's probability of success.

Each individual has to be responsible and accountable for their own actions, and not blame wrongful behavior on the inability to control emotions. Just as a bad temper is not a license to treat others badly, any negative quality cannot be used as an excuse for negative behavior. This not only applies to leaders but every individual, in both a professional and personal capacity. No positive result can come from finger-pointing and passing the blame.

Stressful situations and conflict impact the ability to process information properly. This can then negatively influence the working environment and soul of the ship. How an individual handles any given situation will determine whether it results in a positive or negative atmosphere. It is very important to think before acting and to then react intellectually, not emotionally.

Nobody wants to be on a ship where the crew's judgment is impaired due to a bad attitude

~ FOAMSHIP ~
Shaping Organizational Success

2. Confidence

Confidence is a person's deep-seated belief that they are competent in what they are doing. A feeling of self-efficacy in the ability to perform and to achieve goals is what keeps individuals moving forward during moments of doubt or difficulty. Confidence is demonstrated by speaking clearly and firmly while being courteous and not by bragging or behaving arrogantly.

True confidence assists in fulfilling the basic human need for security. On an internal level, crew members need to feel secure about their jobs. On an external level, customers, suppliers, and partners perceive this confidence as an assurance of the ship's ability to deliver on its promises. During difficult times this confidence enables the ship to perform like a duck – serene on the outside while paddling effusively beneath the surface of the water. A true FOAMSHIP must gleam with mature confidence, regardless of the weather.

No one boards a ship whose crew says: "Wow, I've never been on one of these before!"

3. Courage

In today's world, and business climate, it's crucial for captains and crews to find the courage to try new things. It's necessary to take calculated risks with ideas, strategies, and resources. Listening to logic is essential, but it's also important to listen to intuition. A healthy approach to mistakes and conflicts, both internally and externally, is to see them as sources of opportunities and positive change. A good captain must not only be courageous themselves but also promote, support, and reward courage within their crew.

Courage is boldness minus foolishness

4. Creativity

Competition is fierce in most markets these days. This means that it simply isn't viable for an organization to offer precisely the same product or service endlessly. To compete effectively, it's imperative to innovate and bring new products and services to the marketplace. Nature is a prime example of how important this is because in the natural world, that which does not grow, dies.

In the fast-paced world of business, creativity is a competitive advantage. An effective crew consists of resourceful individuals who think and act, instead of simply reacting. Creativity can be sparked by the right environment and, as human beings, all individuals have the capacity to be creative if the conditions are conducive to expressing ideas. Innovation is born from creativity and this enhances the ship's ability to compete.

Creative minds breed innovative ideas

5. Detail-Oriented

One of the main differences between market-leading companies and those that just play "follow-the-leader" is their level of attention to detail. In an era when the competition is often very close, it's the little things that differentiate one product or service from another. This means that crew members need understand that every detail is important and can be the deciding factor between success and failure.

Quality is in the details and this makes it a very valuable business differentiator. Consider a ship as an example of how little things can make a big difference. Imagine that the ship has one million parts and 1% of these parts are of inferior quality – that means that there are 10,000 parts that are likely to fail. The failure of a single part of the ship can lead to it sinking, so it's vital to pay attention to details and strive for the highest possible levels of quality.

Attention to detail is the hallmark of excellence

6. Fun and Enthusiasm

The journey to any destination is seldom a straight line, so it's necessary to enjoy the journey as well. This can be encouraged by working environments that promote high levels of pride and optimism. Energy is contagious so it is in the best interest of everyone on board to foster positive energy. It is a natural part of life for every individual to have ups and downs, both personally and professionally. Fun and enthusiasm can be incorporated into work activities in a variety of ways and this creates a more nurturing

~ FOAMSHIP ~
Shaping Organizational Success

environment. Constant challenges to try new and different ideas can result in innovative improvements, but it's important to set attainable goals and take the time to celebrate achievements and the successful meeting of challenges. These accomplishments create a "we can" atmosphere which builds momentum and carries the ship steadily towards its destination.

Taking some time for the souls on board the FOAMSHIP to "play" amongst themselves or with customers and suppliers provides a reminder of life's higher purpose and develops stronger human relationships. A ship must replenish its "fun reserves" along the way or its engines and people will wear out prematurely. Nurturing the lighter elements of human nature will enhance and increase the positive energy of the soul.

Regenerate regularly – Work hard and play hard

7. Humor

A good and honest laugh has a significant therapeutic effect. Psychological studies have proven that laughter triggers a chemical reaction in the brain and body that results in the individual feeling more relaxed and at ease.

Humor is an antidote to stress and there is no doubt that stress is a constant in the working world. However, different people handle stress differently. When rough seas start to take a toll on the ship, there is nothing quite like a good laugh to help the captain and crew to unwind a little. Taking that moment to relax also serves as a reminder that people should work to live, not live to work. Keeping life in perspective assists in maintaining a healthy work-life balance and this enables the ability to enjoy both work and life to the fullest.

Those who laugh, last

8. Learning

Knowledge is the capacity for action, and to continue sailing forward in this information age, an organization must never stop learning. Complacency and a "know it all" attitude are likely to doom a ship and all souls on board.

~ FOAMSHIP ~
Shaping Organizational Success

A successful workplace adopts a mentality of continuous learning and feedback, which enables the ability to learn from all angles and perspectives.

It's necessary to constantly search inside and outside of the ship to seek ways to improve and meet high standards for growth. Today's fast-paced business environment requires vigorous entrepreneurial and intrapreneurial minds to take full advantage of opportunities. Fostering an environment where individual and corporate improvement is commonplace allows for a dynamic and stimulating knowledge system.

Knowledge is power

9. Passion

Passion is a very strong emotion and it can assist greatly in getting through the more difficult moments of life. When someone genuinely desires something, they will most likely do whatever it takes to get it. A passionate desire for something, regardless of its nature, is an extremely influential motivator.

Passion is a common characteristic amongst true captains of business. When the business environment presents challenges, a seasoned captain and crew will focus their energy on the tasks at hand, and complete the journey, come rain or shine.

Passion is a key ingredient for success

10. Patience

Business is non-linear and often highly unpredictable. There will always be times when events do not unfold exactly as planned, and this means that the ship's course will need to be periodically re-adjusted to ensure that it reaches the desired destinations.

When exploring the market for business opportunities, not all doors will open on the first knock. The sales process can be lengthy, and many visits to client ports may be required before a sale is finalized. Patience is not only a positive personal virtue but a necessary one in business.

Good things come to those who wait

11. Perseverance

A winner never quits, and a quitter never wins. Obstacles are a part of life and the same is true for business, so it's vital to find ways in which to overcome defeat. In this regard, a business ship is like a long-distance runner who counts on every ounce of mental and physical power to reach the end of the race.

There are numerous paths to success and some are more treacherous than others. Only the toughest and most persevering survive the sometimes-grueling voyage to true success. Assessing the situation and drafting a practical plan of action is key to charging forward across the seas. Self-analyzing successes and failures will assist in turning any temporary failures into a desire to continue the quest.

Colonel Sanders of Kentucky Fried Chicken went to over one thousand places trying to sell his "finger-licking good" recipe before someone finally gave him a chance. Now, that's perseverance!

12. Respect

Every individual has their own views and beliefs about the world around them. This is one of the many things that make each human being unique and valuable. It's important to create an environment that values and respects diverse backgrounds, perspectives, and ideas because this can provide a great source of innovation.

People need to be valued and respected as the individuals they are, and not treated as disposable assets. Respect helps to build confidence and self-esteem. When crew members feel that their captain and organization respect and appreciate them, they will reciprocate that respect and give their best to the ship.

- FOAMSHIP -
Shaping Organizational Success

Mutual respect is mutually beneficial

13. Trust and Integrity

A dictionary definition of trust is a "firm belief in the reliability, truth, ability, or strength of someone or something." Strong relationships of all kinds are built on this belief that someone is reliable, truthful, able, or strong. Trust is a valuable asset that can generate great returns, but it is also very fragile. It typically takes a considerable amount of time to build trust, and only a fraction of a second to destroy it. Integrity is "the quality of being honest and having strong moral principles" and this makes it a key factor in developing trust.

An organization's reputation relies on its integrity and trustworthiness. Negative opinions tend to spread quicker and further than positive ones, so an organization needs to develop a strongly positive reputation to stay afloat. If a ship, its captain, and its crew are known to be steady, reliable, honest, and true to their word, customers will be more likely to remain loyal, even when mistakes are made. Just as no person is perfect all the time, neither is any organization. But integrity supports a good reputation and this enables customers to trust the organizational ship to deliver.

"The two most important things in any company do not
appear on its balance sheet: its reputation and its people."

Henry Ford

To build a strong foundation of trust requires honesty and consistency in both words and actions, as well as the alignment of the two. Promises are easy to make, but if they are not kept and delivered on, the trust will be broken. True success cannot be achieved without trust and integrity.

Trust is priceless – it cannot be bought

14. Teamwork

Leadership and teamwork are concepts that strongly influence the way that business is conducted these days. Studies from various disciplines have

76

proven repeatedly that "power in unity" is as true in business as it is in sports. However, immature perspectives must be removed from the equation when this concept is applied in a corporate setting if it is to succeed. The focus cannot be on someone winning and someone losing. Instead, it's essential to seek win-win or no-lose methodologies, where all parties involved will benefit.

The strength of human relationships will ultimately play an important role in determining how competitive an organization proves to be. Building healthy business relationships with crew members is just as important as maintaining strong customer relationships. The growth of alliances, not only with suppliers but also competitors, demonstrates that teamwork is a very powerful force. Teamwork evokes synergy which enables all parties to benefit from a cohesive and cooperative effort.

"No one can whistle a symphony. It takes a whole orchestra to play it." - H.E. Luccock

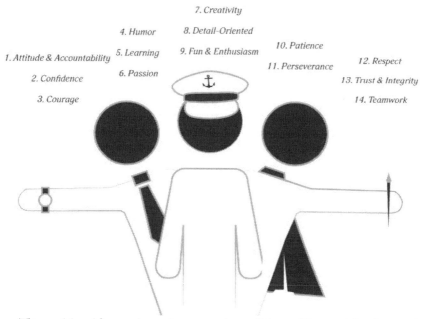

7. Creativity

4. Humor   8. Detail-Oriented

1. Attitude & Accountability   5. Learning   9. Fun & Enthusiasm   10. Patience   12. Respect

2. Confidence   6. Passion   11. Perseverance   13. Trust & Integrity

3. Courage   14. Teamwork

These 14 wide-ranging virtues and qualities will nourish the soul. Although not every company, entity, or individual will exhibit each and every

- FOAMSHIP -
Shaping Organizational Success

one of these characteristics, they are traits that should be nurtured. Leaders and individuals alike should promote and encourage these virtues in the working environment, whilst striving to instill them within themselves.

Equity, Diversity, and Inclusion

The concept of Equity, Diversity, and Inclusion (EDI) is commonly considered to be part of best practices for any organization – in both the for-profit and nonprofit worlds.

Equity – refers to the fair treatment, access, advancement, and opportunity for all people.

Diversity – considers the ways in which people differ, including diversity of thought.

Inclusion – creates an environment where all are welcomed, respected, supported, and valued.

There are numerous reasons to promote tailoring EDI to a business setting, and any true FOAMSHIP captain will see the value and benefit of embracing this concept aboard their organizational ship. Firstly, there is the moral/social aspect whereby everyone has the opportunity to contribute to a "society", the organization, which in turn becomes richer and improved by everyone's contributions. From an economic perspective, diverse talent pools improve society as a whole, and this is equally true in business. Diversity of thought also greatly enhances innovation and this is essential for remaining competitive.

Including a diverse talent pool provides the skills necessary to better serve communities and customers. This increases marketability, competitiveness, and reputation. In general, diversity has been proven to bring about better solutions to society's problems, obstacles, and challenges. Adopting EDI within an organization will result in a stronger and more competent crew, whose efforts will keep the ship on course to success.

Staying the Course

Intangible elements are slippery creatures to grasp for the purpose of measurement. Although Soul itself cannot be measured, there are many ways to gauge the overall atmosphere and working environment of an organization. Just as the ship's barometer measures atmospheric pressure to predict short-term weather changes, so the Soul dashboard measures various elements to predict the environmental conditions of the ship's soul.

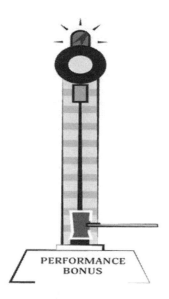

PERFORMANCE
BONUS

Performance Bonus: Within a true FOAMSHIP organization, good performance is rewarded with benefits such as cash, days off, trips, perks, etc. Therefore, a beneficial gauge on the Soul dashboard would be one measuring the rewards that the captain has distributed amongst the officers and shipmates.

The HR department plays an important role in designing the reward gauge, as well as providing the data necessary to feed this meter on the Soul dashboard. Regardless of the nature of the reward and whether it's paid out monthly, quarterly, or annually, the performance bonus is a very useful tool at the captain's disposal.

Sam knows that demonstrating appreciation for the efforts made by her officers and shipmates assists in nourishing her ship's soul and maintaining a motivated and productive crew.

EMPLOYEE SATISFACTION

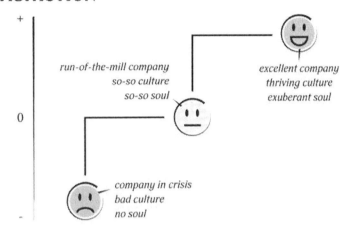

Culture: It can be argued that a captain's primary task is culture management. Many organizations believe that keeping employees happy will translate into happy customers – and happy customers mean a consistent fuel supply. So, just as Marketing conducts external customer satisfaction surveys, management should conduct internal employee satisfaction surveys.

This can be performed as a formal or informal process, but the end goal will always be to gain a sense of the true "pulse" of the organization's soul. The measurement tools used to gauge the crew's satisfaction levels can be as simple as selecting a sad, neutral, or happy face, or a more complex 1-10 scale. The HR department will prove to be invaluable when designing and implementing this gauge. A positive organizational culture and satisfied crew are essential for a sturdy ship and triumphant voyage.

SOCIAL IMPACT

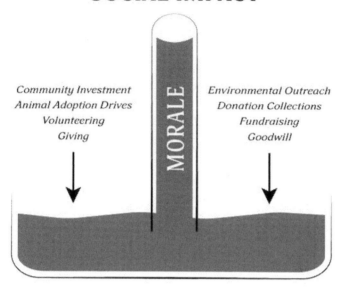

Social Impact: Offering employees paid time off to volunteer for causes they are passionate about has become a very popular company perk. This type of benefit is often referred to as Corporate Social Responsibility (CSR) and it can take on many shapes, not only volunteering. Depending on the organization, it could be in the form of trips to help a developing country, providing resources to underserved communities, teaching classes abroad, matched financial contributions, and a wide range of other forms of assistance.

Some organizations truly go the extra mile and offer ways to give back that are tailored to the employee, and not the company. That shows a true commitment to striving for a positive social impact. The most popular options for giving back in an employee-centric environment are:

♦ Volunteering for a cause that the employee is personally passionate about, not one chosen by the organization.
♦ Pro-bono skills-based volunteering allows individuals to offer their services in areas specific to their personal skills or career-based knowledge and abilities. e.g., a crew member working in Sales or Marketing can assist with fundraising for a nonprofit, or a software programmer can help an entity with its programming needs.

♦ Employee-inspired giving enables the crew members of a ship to request donations to their favorite charities or causes that they are passionate about supporting.

Engaging the soul of the ship with the soul of the community is a win-win situation. Companies that engage this way and adopt a positive approach to CSR benefit in multi-dimensional ways, such as:

- Increased sales
- Customer loyalty
- Higher levels of employee satisfaction
- Greater employee commitment
- Increased productivity
- Greater appeal to highly skilled employees
- Enhanced brand reputation
- Community goodwill

Sam monitors Bright Beacon Ltd.'s social impact gauge as a means of checking that the soul of her ship is positive and healthy. She knows her crew members are enriched by giving back to society in thoughtful and practical ways. The increased energy onboard a FOAMSHIP organizational vessel is noticeable when the social impact is positive.

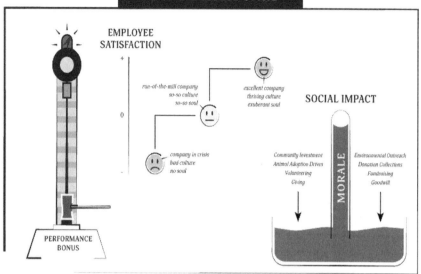

The benefits of a work environment in which business and human elements operate in synchronized harmony cannot be emphasized enough. The culture that emanates from a ship is a direct reflection of the captain, officers, and shipmates that make up an organization. Soul has a significant impact on the overall atmosphere of an organization and it will grow or deteriorate according to the care and attention it receives.

Now that Sam and Fran have a clear understanding of Bright Beacon Ltd.'s soul, it is necessary to consider how **S**oul and **H**eading link people to purpose aboard the FOAMSHIP. Plot the course and sail on!

Examples: Souls

Consult the FOAMSHIP online case library (www.foamship.com/cases) to learn from extraordinary captains and hone your own captain skills. These exemplary companies offer valuable real-life examples of how to nourish and nurture the organization's Souls.

Key Points: Souls

Review the key discussion points for this chapter.

SOULS

The collective human energy aboard our ship that:

- Provides rational and analytical capabilities, as well as intuitive and creative genius.
- Gives the organization meaning and links people to purpose.
- Can be cultivated to be a tremendous source of innovative ideas.
- Is a direct reflection of our most differentiating asset – our people's spirit.

~ FOAMSHIP ~
Shaping Organizational Success

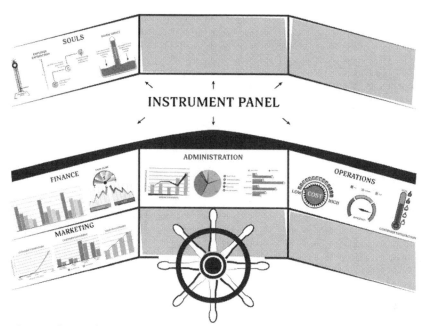

Remember to keep a close eye on your instrument panel to monitor the gauges of each FOAMSHIP component's dashboard.

Pulpit: Souls

Use these questions to hone your skills in applying the FOAMSHIP model in practice.

1. Do you enjoy your job? Do the other crew members enjoy their jobs? Why, or why not?
2. How would you describe the spirit within your organization?
3. Brainstorm ways in which your organization can better link its purpose with its people.
4. Consider ways to nurture and nourish the soul of your organization.
5. What personal qualities do you possess that positively impact your organization's soul?

- FOAMSHIP -
Shaping Organizational Success

8. HEADING IN THE RIGHT DIRECTION

"If you don't know where you are going, any road will get you there."

Lewis Carroll

Sam knows that a clear understanding of a company's strengths and the climate it operates in is critical to an organization's success. In business jargon, what an enterprise excels at is known as its core competency, which might be logistics, product design, convenience, standardization, or one of many other potential fields. The Heading or direction of an organization is traditionally known as the Vision of the company. Fran has suggested that Bright Beacon Ltd.'s Vision Statement may need to be updated to align with the changes and improvements that have been made since adopting the FOAMSHIP model.

Vision statements are those futuristic nuggets of wisdom that are often casually observed on elaborate plaques in corporate lobbies or in glossy annual reports. A few choice, lofty words about what the organization strives to achieve as it toils away towards the future. Yet ask any employee to state what those few vision words are and more often than not a blank stare will be the response. This is either because the crew members on board that ship don't know what the vision is, or because they have not been driven towards it.

Most of the time, the vision is set by top management or business consultants, gets framed for the lobby of the building, and that's where the integration of the vision into the organization ends. Few ever ask:

- Does the vision truly reflect the goals of the organization?
- Does it align with the company's approach to business?
- Is the vision challenging but realistically achievable?
- Is it too far-reaching to be feasible?
- Will the individual identify with the company's vision?

Communicating the Captain's Vision is critical to the organization's success – it sets the Heading.

A vast number of books have been written about defining corporate visions and there are a seemingly endless number of consultants teaching companies how to articulate it. Far too many organizations have generic standardized vision statements that tend to include phrases such as:

"We will be the leader in our field."
"We will be the best providers of XYZ services in the world."
"We will be the global leader in gizmos and gadgets."

It is clear to see that these vision statements may be unrealistic and don't offer any indication of how the organization plans to deliver on these promises. Generically grandiose vision statements can do more harm than good. That approach can negatively affect the customer's impression of the organization because a vision statement based on "fluff" does not instill a sense of trust or confidence in the company. It is also very difficult for crew members to get on board and commit to a vision statement that they either don't understand or can't believe in.

It's a common but outdated trend for corporate vision statements to focus solely on the importance of exciting the customer or bending over backward to make clients feel valued. Although providing for the wants and needs of the customer is important, it's just as necessary to take care of the crew members who serve the customers. Sam recalls what she learned about Soul, and realizes that promoting an atmosphere of enthusiasm amongst her crew will create an environment where they will, in turn, excite the customer.

Heading towards the Vision

The journey towards the vision is seldom a straight line and guiding an organizational ship is not a "one size fits all" activity. Adopting a generalized vision statement like "Being the best in the world" makes it difficult to obtain the buy-in and commitment of the crew. In fact, trying to follow a generic vision statement is the equivalent of trying to hit a moving target.

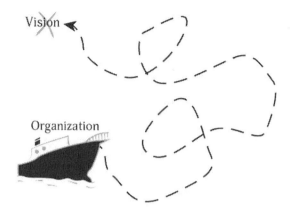

To straighten this path, the FOAMSHIP model utilizes the concept of Heading to translate vision into action. While vision is subjective, Heading is a more concrete nautical term, implying motion in a specific direction, which crew members can understand, embrace, and commit to.

Aboard a sea vessel, the captain and crew trace the route to follow on navigational charts. With global positioning instrumentation, they read the data to estimate and plot the best course between their current position and the desired destination. With the FOAMSHIP methodology, tools are used to measure, organize, align, and synchronize people and resources to ensure that the ship is heading in the right direction.

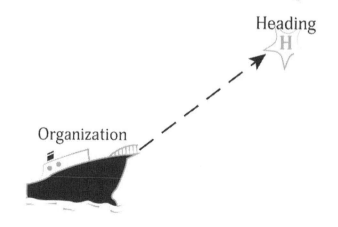

All Hands on Deck

To plot the best route from the present location to the future port, Sam knows that these questions must be answered by Bright Beacon Ltd.'s vision statement:

- How do we want the organization to interact with customers?
- What culture do we want to promote within the organization, and how will it affect the lives of the crew?
- What impact do we want the organization to have in its field?
- How can our ship remain competitive at sea whilst adding value to the world around it?

Considering and identifying these elements will provide a strong foundation from which to develop a vision statement that is a true reflection of the ship's organizational objectives. Although it's necessary to customize according to an organization's purpose and needs, there are important aspects to bear in mind when developing a vision statement.

Heading with a Purpose – determine the purpose of the organization's existence to ensure that the vision statement captures the ship's interests and strategic direction.

Keep it Simple – vision statements should be crafted using clear, concise, and common language that's easily understood and not padded with unsubstantial "fluff".

Communicate Clearly – the vision needs to be communicated clearly to all crew members because a vision statement is useless if no one knows what it is or what it means.

Be Consistent – the captain's vision should be aligned with the business values and goals of the organization to ensure consistency across the ship.

Follow-through – be sure to allocate the necessary time, resources, dedication, and effort required to achieve the vision that's been established.

Feel the Vibe – the vision statement should encapsulate the organization's culture in a way that inspires passion, motivates the crew, and reassures the customers.

Focus on the Future – it's important to understand that the vision statement does not represent where the ship is now, but where it needs to be in the future.

Visualize the Big Picture – the vision statement serves to direct focus towards the desired end-state and provides the crew with a reminder of the ship's Heading.

Reassess, Refresh, Reinvent – vision statements are living documents that must be reviewed, renewed, and revitalized as an organization evolves and grows.

~ FOAMSHIP ~
Shaping Organizational Success

With these points in mind, consider the Heading provided by the vision statement below.

"Our company will be the preferred provider of our product as evidenced by our leadership in market share; provide a challenging and nurturing environment to our employees as demonstrated by their level of job satisfaction and low turnover; as well as provide the largest return to our shareholders in this particular industry."

It's relevant, realistically achievable, focuses on the objectives identified as most important to the organization, aligns with the company culture, notes how success will be measured, and all this is communicated clearly.

<u>Staying the Course</u>
A clear and concise vision will define the direction in which the organizational ship must head to reach its desired destination. With Bright Beacon Ltd.'s route methodically mapped, Sam carefully monitors the associated gauges to ensure that her ship remains on course.

VISION & MISSION

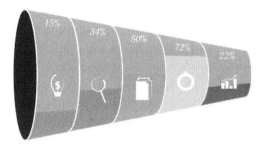

Vision & Mission: Often confused and mistakenly used interchangeably the vision statement and mission statement are, in fact, two separate documents of significant purpose and importance. As discussed, the vision statement defines and describes the desired future destination of the business ship. The mission statement describes what the captain and crew need to do now to reach the destination port.

Elements of the vision statement and mission statement are often combined to document an organization's purpose, goals, culture, and values. The vision and mission statements need to align and support each other. Vision provides the outline and hopes, whilst Mission offers the specifics on how to navigate the journey.

~ FOAMSHIP ~
Shaping Organizational Success

The mission statement is fundamental in the development of strategic organizational goals. Clearly describing the purpose for a business ship's existence, the oceans in which it will compete, and how it will reach its destination port, enables the captain to define goals to support a successful voyage.

Sam monitors Bright Beacon Ltd.'s heading throughout the journey using a Balanced Scorecard. Focused on vision and strategy, this provides a strategic framework to assist in tracking the progress made in achieving the objectives of the mission. A smooth voyage is facilitated by the consistent accomplishment of actionable goals.

SUSTAINABILITY

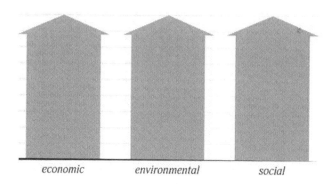

| economic | environmental | social |

TRIPLE BOTTOM LINE

Sustainability: To sail competitively across the oceans of industry an organizational ship must be sustainable. Economic, environmental, and social demands are viewed as the three pillars supporting sustainability. In business, these are often referred to as the "triple bottom line".

93

In the past, the only bottom line that most organizations considered was the economic one, because profit was the sole focus. But a "soul focus" approach is being adopted by an ever-increasing number of organizations around the world. Therefore, to achieve and maintain corporate sustainability, there must be strong management and coordination of social and environmental concerns, as well as the traditional attention to finances.

The vision and mission statements can also assist in supporting the ship's sustainability. Ensuring a clear vision of where the ship is heading and how it will accomplish its mission, keeps the crew focused on the destination and prevents the wastage of resources on opportunities that are not aligned with the objectives.

It's also important to note that the triple bottom line is not solely the responsibility of the captain and officers. Shipmates also have their role to play in contributing to corporate sustainability, such as:

- Recycling initiatives
- Energy-saving recommendations
- Actively reducing waste
- Conservative usage of supplies
- Sourcing eco-friendly materials

Sam and her crew are united in their desire for Bright Beacon Ltd. to achieve long-term sustainability. Monitoring the "triple bottom line" is essential to ensuring a mindful, responsible, and ethical approach to navigating the ship's journey to success.

RELATIONSHIPS

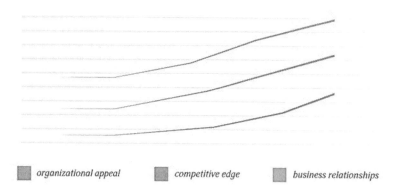

organizational appeal   competitive edge   business relationships

Relationships: Creating and growing strong business relationships, both internally and externally, is critical to success. Heading is very important when it comes to fostering these relationships as it can have a significant impact on how an organization is viewed.

The vision statement can be a vital influencer on both the perspective of the crew and public perception. When the captain's vision is inspirational and shared, it can be a great source of motivation for existing crew members, and also attract valuable new potential officers and shipmates. A clearly defined heading will explain what the organization is working to achieve and this helps current and potential customers, investors, suppliers, and partners to gain a better understanding of the enterprise.

Sam knows that she cannot keep Bright Beacon Ltd. afloat on her own. It would sink without its dedicated crew, loyal customers, reliable suppliers, and ethical partners. Nurturing mutually beneficial relationships in all areas of business can effectively enhance the overall appeal of an organization and increase its competitive edge.

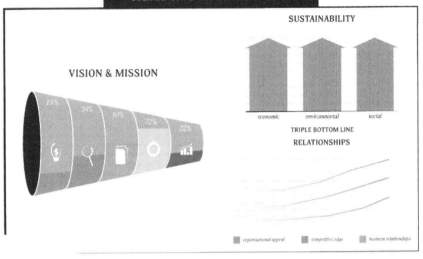

To arrive safely at the desired destination port, the gauges monitoring where the ship is heading can alert the captain and officers to course deviations. Early warnings and alarms triggered by these gauges are like a lighthouse that illuminates obstacles and dangers that could throw the ship off course. Observing the Heading dashboard, in addition to the other dashboards making up the instrument panel, will keep the ship sailing in the right direction.

Agile Heading

It's also vital to remember that if Heading does not take into account the soul of the organization, the ship will never fully realize it's potential. The captain and crew must be inspired to reach the desired destination and some crew members will require more inspiration and motivation than others.

To safely traverse the open seas, the entire organization must also be nimble enough for intricate maneuvers, just like today's modern ships. Modern ships no longer have rudders, which were traditionally used to provide direction, and now make use of azipods instead.

Azipods are swiveling propellers that can be turned in almost any direction, giving the ship thrust in that bearing. They can be visualized as oscillating floor fans attached to the underside of the hull. This nautical advancement enables ships to now "turn on a dime" and perform certain maneuvers without the need for a tugboat. To succeed, organizational ships have to be that agile in the business oceans of today.

FOAMSHIP makes sure that everyone knows where the ship is headed.

When an organization possesses and shares a clear, inspirational Heading, people can feel it and are likely to want to share in it. Crew members are more motivated, loyal, and productive. Suppliers sense it and typically provide better service. Customers buy it in every product or service rendered. People want to be a part of success; just as people want to get into the groove of creative energy surrounding people like Bill Gates of Microsoft, the late Steve Jobs of Apple and Pixar, and Virgin's Richard Branson.

Consider how it feels to be around people who are likable and elicit respect and admiration because of the guidance and insight that they provide. The same feeling will be felt within the organizational environment when the ship is being steered in the right direction and is heading towards success.

Follow the FOAMSHIP star!

97

Examples: Heading

Consult the FOAMSHIP online case library (www.foamship.com/cases) to learn from extraordinary captains and hone your own captain skills. These exemplary companies offer valuable real-life examples of how to plot the most beneficial Heading for an organization.

Key Points: Heading

Review the key discussion points for this chapter.

HEADING

The bright star on the horizon that:

- Is palpable and embraceable by all crew members.
- Provides a clear sense of direction.
- Unites the captain and crew through a shared vision.
- Focuses the energies of all crew members on a common destination.
- Needs to be communicated throughout the voyage to keep crew members aligned.
- Provides reassuring clarity to customers, suppliers, partners, and investors.

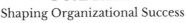

~ FOAMSHIP ~
Shaping Organizational Success

Remember to keep a close eye on your instrument panel to monitor the gauges of each FOAMSHIP component's dashboard.

Pulpit: Heading

Use these questions to hone your skills in applying the FOAMSHIP model in practice.

1. Do you know where your organization is headed? If not, what can be done to clarify the direction?
2. Brainstorm ways to keep your organizational vessel on target to its destination port.
3. Where are you headed in your professional career?
4. Where are you headed in your personal life?

9. INNOVATION DRIVES SUSTAINABILITY

"Not to know is bad; not to wish to know is worse."

- African Proverb

Throughout life, there will always be surprises and perils, and the same is true for business voyages. Dynamic market forces may require sudden changes in speed and direction. How well a ship, its captain, and its crew adapt to these changes will depend on the structural design of the organization. The hull or frame of a ship holds together infrastructure such as electrical wiring, plumbing, tubing, and decks. Purpose dictates the design of a ship's hull. During polar expeditions, there is often the need to open passages through solid ice and this requires a fortified hull. Sleek hulls are designed with speed in mind and are found on competitive sailing vessels. A ship's hull is responsible for keeping the entire entity together… and water out!

Decks are designed around a central core, through which all services and utilities are delivered to passengers and customers at multiple levels, with maximum efficiency and minimum inconvenience. This behind-the-scenes activity takes place swiftly, smoothly, and efficiently if the necessary systems are in place and the crew is knowledgeable about their roles and duties.

Information that flows throughout an organization is a potential source of innovation. While ideas may be plentiful, true innovation occurs when an opportunity to fulfill a customer need is met with a value-added proposition. The commercialization of new technologies, both hi-tech and low-tech, is critical to maintaining an organization's competitive edge, and the long-term sustainability of a business ship.

FOAMSHIP *promotes the flow of information that supports the sharing of knowledge and stimulates the innovation process.*

101

To illustrate the importance of Innovation for navigating unpredictable seas, Sam shares with Fran a cautionary tale from Bright Beacon Ltd.'s very early days. The ship was cruising steadily along what seemed to be smooth seas. Everything appeared to be calm on the horizon. Bright Beacon Ltd.'s largest client had been a loyal customer from the beginning of the journey and their fuel contributions played a significant role in keeping the ship afloat. One day, out of the blue, the client canceled their regular repeat order. No warning, no noticeable blip on the radar, no ringing of alarm bells.

It had been assumed that the customer remained very satisfied with Bright Beacon Ltd.'s product and service delivery. A complacent status quo had set in and the water carrying the ship along had become stagnant. Bright Beacon Ltd. had gotten sluggishly off-course and no one had heard the rocky reef scraping the hull. The customer's needs had changed without anyone on board noticing and a competitor had a better value proposition to offer. As Bright Beacon Ltd.'s captain and crew, everyone aboard the ship shared some level of accountability for the client disembarking.

- ♦ The Marketing crew had continued to offer a long-standing product and service efficiently but without innovation. While the client's needs changed, the crew had slipped into a comfort zone – the arch-enemy of innovation.
- ♦ In the engine room, the Operations crew practiced routines so mechanically that quality levels had dropped. They had failed to continuously improve their processes and procedures.
- ♦ The atmosphere of complacency had led to the Finance crew becoming self-satisfied regarding this single source of fuel. All the ship's fish had been placed in one basket.
- ♦ Administration had been too busy looking at the horizon to see what was happening in the immediate surroundings. Looking towards the future had become the sole focus and it blinded the crew to the present conditions.

Many things had gone wrong. A hole had appeared in the hull and Bright Beacon Ltd. was taking on water. Although the situation was dire and many were sure the ship would sink, Sam and her devoted crew had immediately begun working on solutions to patch the hole and bail out the water. None abandoned ship and Bright Beacon Ltd. had been saved to sail another day. Surviving a disaster that could easily have sunk her ship left Sam determined to avoid, or at least minimize, the possibility of such events being repeated in the future.

All Hands on Deck

To build a robust FOAMSHIP and create an innovative environment calls for a system where information is consistently and methodically shared at all levels. Obstacles must be removed to prevent barriers that can encumber efficient and effective communications. Any crew member onboard the organizational ship should be permitted to run to the bridge to give the captain first-hand knowledge, without tripping over obstacles – human or otherwise.

From the bridge, the Captain doesn't have a 360° view around the ship, and must rely on information received from various sources.

The use of information technology plays a pivotal role in facilitating knowledge management and decision-making. It is also essential for Innovation in terms of products, services, and processes. Utilizing the most beneficial technological tools allows the ship's captain and crew to view data in real-time. This enables proactive measures to be taken before it's too late and ensures that many potential problems and issues are avoided.

Solid technological infrastructure enables efficient management of information for Innovation, providing data at the correct time and place.

Knowledge is the capacity for action, and to sail ahead in the world of business an organizational ship must be action-oriented. Experience gained from each expedition needs to be translated into "repositories" of intellectual capital that benefits future journeys. This knowledge is extremely valuable as it assists in the planning of future voyages and teaches new crew members the lessons that have already been learned by others through experience.

The amount of information available can be overwhelming to the crew members of any ship. However, Sam believes an organization that encourages team learning and a shared Heading has the capacity to absorb and handle vast amounts of information to support Innovation. The potential to innovate will be a significant competitive edge that strengthens the hull of Bright Beacon Ltd.

103

~ FOAMSHIP ~
Shaping Organizational Success

"Knowledge maps" are created from information gathered along voyages to enable seasoned crew members to chart new courses, and to accelerate training new crew members.

Facilitating the continuous flow of information is a never-ending effort required for an innovative environment. Crew members need to be refreshed with training in subject matters related to their roles. Benchmarking best practices enables the crew to maintain its edge over the competition. Management must ensure that there are unobstructed, smooth-flowing channels of communication to keep the crew informed. This all makes for a more knowledgeable, dedicated, and happy crew.

Crew members take pride in a ship that supports professional and personal growth through acquiring new knowledge and skills.

To determine whether Bright Beacon Ltd. promotes and supports an innovative environment, Sam and Fran compiled a list of questions to consider:

- Does the ship have systems in place for converting suggestions and ideas into actions?
- How are ideas implemented to affect real change?
- Is innovation embraced as a way to increase competitiveness?
- Are the crew members reassured that no ideas are "dumb"?
- Are unorthodox ideas encouraged or ridiculed?
- Is there a learning or content management system in place to capture institutional knowledge and experience?
- How do values and quality affect decisions relating to new products, services, and/or processes?
- How are innovative initiatives communicated throughout the ship?
- Is an organizational culture of innovation encouraged?

Not only is it necessary for Sam and her crew to achieve an innovative environment, but the spirit of innovation must also be maintained as the ship progresses along its journeys.

<u>Staying the Course</u>

Many different metrics can be used to measure innovation within a company, and these vary greatly according to the industry in which the organization operates. A firm specializing in technology products or services may monitor the number of patents produced in a given period. Pharmaceutical companies will closely track the expenditures relating to Research and Development (R&D). A business selling household hygiene and sanitation products is going to need to watch the success rate of a new soap added to their product line.

Sam has customized her Innovation dashboard to measure the metrics important to Bright Beacon Ltd.'s business voyage. Making sure that the gauges offered a true reflection of what must be monitored included seeking insight and input from Fran, the crew, and the customers. Innovation begins with ideas and a good captain knows that ideas can come from many sources – particularly those individuals involved with providing and purchasing the products or services.

NEW PRODUCTS/SERVICES LAUNCHED

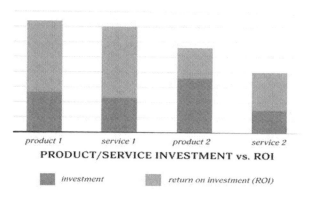

PRODUCT/SERVICE INVESTMENT vs. ROI

investment   return on investment (ROI)

New Products Launched: A new product always begins its life cycle as an idea. The idea could come from paying attention to the wants and needs of the customer, or a crew member who has noticed a gap in the market, or supplier trends, or even by spotting a potential improvement that could be made to an existing product. New products and services are also very often launched in direct response to what is being offered by the competition.

Approving an idea for a new product or service triggers the development process and this can be a long journey that requires dedication and follow-through. For various reasons, many ideas are discarded before they can be

realized, so when a new product completes the journey from conception to realization, it demonstrates a commitment to innovation and a strong belief in that particular new offering.

Launching new products and services requires a significant investment. This means that any new offering must pass feasibility and viability studies to ensure that it is worth pursuing. It's vital to the sustainability of any organization to avoid wasting valuable resources on launching products or services that have not been properly thought-out, researched, and planned. Discontinuing products or services that don't yield a worthwhile Return on Investment (ROI) prevents a prolonged drain on these resources.

Fran helps Sam to monitor the launch of Bright Beacon Ltd.'s new products because he's in direct daily contact with shipmates and customers. The feedback he obtains assists in determining how the new product is being received. This flow of communication from customers and shipmates is essential for pinpointing any necessary adjustments or improvements that are required. The level of innovation within an organization impacts significantly on the success rate of new products or services.

COMMUNICATION CHANNELS

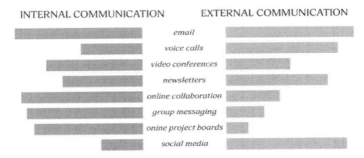

INTERNAL COMMUNICATION   EXTERNAL COMMUNICATION

- email
- voice calls
- video conferences
- newsletters
- online collaboration
- group messaging
- onine project boards
- social media

Communication Channels: Communication and innovation go hand-in-hand. With the advancement of modern technology comes the ability to communicate in a wider variety of ways and this can both promote and support innovation within an organization.

Clear and consistent communication throughout the ship is imperative for the smooth flow of information and this is key for the success of innovative initiatives. Establishing multiple communication channels provides an array of alternatives for the captain and crew to effectively share ideas, information, and knowledge. This diversity in the communication options available to businesses today offers many advantages, such as:

- Easy online collaboration tools
- Virtual workspaces and meeting rooms
- Quick and effective sharing
- Corporate webcasts and podcasts
- Ability to send text, images, audio, and video
- Voice and video calling
- Online project boards
- Group messaging apps
- Social media platforms
- Real-time global communication

Efficient communication is a core component of a successful voyage as it ensures that all individuals involved are kept in the loop. For an innovative initiative to succeed, all crew members must be on board and this requires them to remain informed. Just as everyone needs to share the captain's vision of where the ship is heading, they also need to know and understand the strategies in place for the implementation of innovative initiatives.

Another important factor is to ensure that all communication is consistent and aligned. Too often the internal and external communications of an organization are mismatched. This can have a severely negative impact on crew members as it is confusing and demotivating to be given one message, while the public is given a differing message.

As captain, Sam must choose the correct communication channels for her ship's specific needs. This then changes and evolves with time and can be affected by many elements such as what stage of the journey the ship is at, and which port it will call on next. Gauging which communication channels are favored by Bright Beacon Ltd.'s crew, customers, suppliers, and partners is crucial in promoting and supporting innovation efforts.

INNOVATIVE ENVIRONMENT

Innovative Environment: A well-planned, consistent communication strategy is also necessary for the creation and development of an innovative working environment. Organizational culture is a vital part of the FOAMSHIP model and this includes implementing and fostering a culture of innovation within the workplace. An innovative culture enables the implementation of innovative ideas. Having great ideas is a start, but for innovation to truly flourish the organizational culture of the ship must support the pursuit of new endeavors. When an organization actively encourages an innovative environment, it results in an extensive range of benefits, including:

- Ground-breaking new products and/or services
- Competitive advantage
- Increased sales
- Motivated crew members
- Higher levels of productivity
- Improved processes and procedures
- Greater customer satisfaction
- Enhanced job satisfaction
- Career development
- Corporate sustainability

The importance of innovation resulting from internal process improvements cannot be emphasized enough. An example of this is a better use of technology to expedite the reporting of results in Finance, Operations, Administration, and Marketing. Another example is introducing wellness practices to promote a healthier and more productive work environment. Whatever form innovation takes, the goal is to build a better and stronger organizational vessel with an innovative environment.

~ FOAMSHIP ~
Shaping Organizational Success

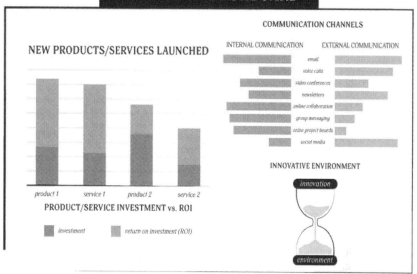

As discussed, best practices can assist the ship and crew to maintain a competitive edge. These can vary greatly, depending on the nature of the business and the arena in which it competes, but the benefits of discovering and exploring them can be significant. Sam strives to ensure that Bright Beacon Ltd. adopts the most relevant best practices relating to its information management, knowledge creation, and culture of innovation.

Communication of financial performance

Companies that can provide nearly instant snapshots of their financial performance shortly after closing their books earn increased financial credibility and improved stakeholder relationships. Consistently communicating this information throughout a voyage promotes transparency, honesty, and integrity.

Communication between captains and crews

The most innovative companies are often those where the upper-level executives take the time to communicate directly with their employees. There are many ways to facilitate this such as casual luncheons, formal employee roundtables, and informal conversations. Although Sam trusts her officers to provide her with valuable crew feedback, she also knows that there is a wealth of ideas to be uncovered by talking directly to the shipmates herself. Adopting a flat organization approach to communication removes intermediaries and promotes direct communication between all souls on board. This enables Sam to gain a personal feel for what is happening on the decks of her ship, and what opportunities for innovation are being suggested.

Consistent sharing of information

To achieve a successful culture of innovation, a concerted effort must be made to ensure that information is consistently available to all crew members and other stakeholders. This can be done in a very wide variety of ways and greatly strengthens the relationship between employees and management. Innovation cannot take root and flourish without information.

Continuous skills development

Implementing formalized training and/or mentorship programs ensures the continuous upward development of the ship's crew. This demonstrates to crew members that they are important and valued and that their career progression is supported and encouraged. Today's shipmate is tomorrow's captain. Increased knowledge and ability also lead to innovation as crew members become more adept at recommending and developing new products, services, and ways of working.

Sharing and celebrating successes

When a ship's success is shared and celebrated with all crew members it shows that they are considered valuable members of the business expedition. This goes a long way to building the type of loyalty that reinforces the collective Soul and makes it unshakeable in times of turmoil. Strong leadership and a devoted crew can prepare a ship for any passage.

Taking the initiative to innovate

Crew members have differing levels of self-initiative. Some only need to be given an objective and they will find a way to achieve it, whilst others may need more specific step-by-step instructions on how to reach the same goal. This means that directions to the crew must be delivered in detail that is sufficient to enable everyone to accomplish their tasks. A company culture that encourages crew members to take greater initiative will create a cycle of continuous innovation.

Information for innovation

Captains are not solely responsible for the task of building a solid knowledge infrastructure. The entire crew shares the responsibility of contributing to the information-sharing approach that is essential for innovation. Each individual crew member is an important conduit for the flow of information throughout the entire organizational vessel. Communication of ideas, suggestions, and recommendations must be encouraged in all areas of business.

As can be seen, communication is a core component required for the creation of an innovative environment because it facilitates the vital flow of information. However, developing and nurturing a culture of innovation

within an organization requires on-going consideration and effort. To be truly successful, an organization must also be sure to customize all innovative initiatives to meet its specific objectives and goals.

With that knowledge firmly in mind, you're almost seaworthy and ready to set sail!

Examples: Innovation

Consult the FOAMSHIP online case library (www.foamship.com/cases) to learn from extraordinary captains and hone your own captain skills. These exemplary companies offer valuable real-life examples that explore how to lead by Innovation.

Key Points: Innovation

Review the key discussion points for this chapter.

INNOVATION

Our ship's ability to innovate:

- Facilitates the flow of information and the sharing of data throughout the organization.
- Enables effective communication between captains, officers, and shipmates at all levels.
- Captures valuable knowledge for future journeys, thus increasing organizational learning and information-sharing.

Remember to keep a close eye on your instrument panel to monitor the gauges of each FOAMSHIP component's dashboard.

Pulpit: Innovation

Use these questions to hone your skills in applying the FOAMSHIP model in practice.

1. Have you experienced a situation that resulted from a breakdown in professional or personal communication?
2. How were these situations handled, and how could this be improved by using FOAMSHIP concepts and principles?
3. Are you provided with all the information required to do your job properly?
4. Are you encouraged to seek innovative solutions or improvements?
5. Are you rewarded for an innovative approach?

~ FOAMSHIP ~
Shaping Organizational Success

6. Does your organization actively strive for an innovation-friendly environment?
7. Consider ways you can improve the "infrastructure hull" of information, knowledge, and innovation within your organization or personal life.
8. Based on what you've learned about communication aboard the FOAMSHIP, how can you become a better communicator and innovator?

10. PASSAGE ACROSS THE HIGH SEAS

"Greatness is not in where we stand, but in what direction we are moving. We must sail sometimes with the wind, and sometimes against it - but sail we must, and not drift, nor lie at anchor."

Oliver Wendell Holmes, Jr.

Surveying her ship, Sam feels that Bright Beacon Ltd. is now ready to navigate across the high seas, but she wonders whether she and her crew are ready.

Passage is the path taken to reach a particular destination. However, each voyage along the path is unique, with its own challenges, adventures, and learning experiences. The expression "a rite of passage" refers to rituals or events undertaken to graduate to a new level of competency or maturity. Successfully achieving the next level indicates being ready for the next stage of life's journey. For example, many tribes in Africa have rites of passage ceremonies to mark the transition from childhood into adulthood. Similarly, aboard the FOAMSHIP, conquering opportunities helps the crew to "earn their stripes" and grow in knowledge and rank.

Passage relies on preparation. When contemplating a voyage that is about to be undertaken, many questions and doubts will arise. After all, seafaring is not for the faint of heart. The captain and crew must be aware of all the internal and external conditions, the limitations, risks, opportunities, resources, challenges, and potential rewards. These were explored in the FOAMSHIP areas already discovered, and the focus must now be on the ship's Passage.

As a captain, Sam knows how crucial it is to keep careful watch over her ship's passage and prepare for what's ahead. A prime example of the importance of this can be seen in crossing the Panama Canal. Many of the ships that travel this route are over 1,000 feet long by over 100 feet wide

(over 300m long by over 30m wide). The Panama Canal's locks have a maximum width of 110 feet (33m) and 83 feet (25m) of depth. This means that a ship's captain and crew cannot only begin thinking about maneuvering into the canal upon arrival. The ship must be prepared and positioned well ahead of time and slowed down to the appropriate speed — it takes miles to slow down a moving ship.

When a ship enters the canal, it sometimes has merely inches of clearance on each side as it traverses its way along the 51 miles (82km) from one end of the canal to the other. However, the canal presents an opportunity that benefits the ship and its passengers and this makes the helmsmanship challenge worth the risk. The benefit of crossing the Panama Canal is that it connects the Atlantic Ocean to the Pacific Ocean, thus shortening the trip between New York and San Franco by 7,872 miles (12 668km)! This significant reduction in distance has the immediate benefit of reducing the cost and time associated with this particular journey. Substantially minimizing the resources required enables a higher return on investment for the voyage. That's smart sailing.

However, it's wise to remember that crossing a particular passage successfully does not guarantee a triumphant crossing of the next one. Each journey is different and a new learning experience.

~ FOAMSHIP ~
Shaping Organizational Success

When an organization undergoes a thorough FOAMSHIP analysis, the process will reveal how well the organizational vessel is moving towards its goal destination. Key indicators such as speed-to-market, resource utilization, and financial data tell the captain and crew how swiftly the ship is traveling along its passage, whether it is still on course, if it's sinking, or just plain dead in the water. An ongoing FOAMSHIP examination ensures continuous organizational improvement.

Throughout each passage, a FOAMSHIP organization strives to operate at peak effectiveness and efficiency in the pursuit of its objectives and goals. Similarly, each individual soul aboard the ship learns and grows from the new experiences and challenges presented by each passage. At the end of a voyage, the organization and its crew members are stronger, more competent, and better equipped to face future endeavors.

Every passage is an opportunity to increase personal and organizational value.

<u>All Hands on Deck</u>

Preparation is essential for any journey. When considering a new voyage, the captain and crew must take stock of the current situation, and get ready for the passage ahead. Although each organization's pre-sail checklist will be customized to its specific needs and the goals that must be achieved, various elements can be helpful to any ship making its way across the oceans of industry.

Atten-hut!

Onboard a FOAMSHIP vessel, every action and activity is inspired by the ship's Heading and contributes to guiding the ship in the right direction. The captain and crew must ensure that all work offers value to the functions within the organization. Always remembers that everything impacts all organizational components of the business ship. Pay attention and focus.

Set the Course

The captain is responsible for identifying the ship's goals and setting the destination coordinates for the route required to reach the desired port. Rigorous analysis of customer needs and a close examination of the environmental conditions provides the information required to set the course.

Everyone onboard the ship must know where it is heading, without ambiguity. Information must flow smoothly in all directions throughout the voyage to keep everyone on track. When expected situations or passage deviations arise, the captain and crew of a FOAMSHIP vessel react with focus and efficiency.

Quantify the goals

It must be determined and noted how success will be measured in terms of the specific goals that have been set. Identifying the criteria that must be met to consider the goals achieved is an essential part of quantifying the objectives of the journey. Knowing what the goals are, and what is required to achieve them, will ensure that the captain and crew know where to focus their efforts. Progress towards these goals will indicate whether the ship is being navigated along the correct passage.

Spot the horizon

To provide a focal point to work towards and a clear end-point, it is beneficial to pinpoint the goal-date. This is the desired point in time by which the journey's objectives must be met. When this has been reached, the ship's vision and mission should be re-evaluated before launching the next voyage.

~ FOAMSHIP ~
Shaping Organizational Success

Load 'er up and let go

Just as the ship needs to load up with fresh supplies, additional shipmates, and replenished resources, the captain and crew also load up with fresh knowledge and skills to assist in future voyages. This can be achieved in many ways such as the experience gained during prior endeavors, training investments, personal growth, and a focus on professional development.

It's also necessary to unload any excess baggage such as bad habits that will slow the ship down like barnacles on the hull. The captain, officers, and shipmates must all be in tip-top shape before embarking on the next passage crossing.

Inspire the crew

It's absolutely imperative to set desirable goals that are in the best interests of all involved. This will create and share a vision that ignites the crew's passion while focusing the collective Soul energy on heading in the right direction. This inspiration will shine like a beacon for the ship to steadily follow along its passage. An inspired crew is a motivated crew, and a motivated crew is typically a successful crew.

Drill, drill, drill!

Practice, practice, practice! The whole crew must function like a team and practice makes perfect. All souls on board the ship need to know their specific roles and stations for normal voyages, as well as for emergency situations. Running drills occasionally will assist in preparing for potential conditions that could arise, so that nothing is left to chance. It's never advisable to wait for the iceberg to be in sight before figuring out what to do about it. Even a seasoned captain and crew with a good sense of how to keep a ship running smoothly needs to remain prepared. Complacency can sink a ship.

Man your stations

When the course has been set and it's all systems go, the captain calls for the crew to man their stations. All hands on deck! This is the moment when the captain and crew must commit to the journey and give it their all. Successful companies continuously raise the performance bar from voyage to voyage. If a ship is only as good as its last successful voyage, it's essential to return from each venture in improved condition and with a crew that has been enhanced by the expedition. Stay on top of each journey and make the most of it.

Blow that horn and go!

The captain and crew are ready, the course has been set, the anchor has been hoisted, and the ship is finally heading out to sea. Full speed ahead towards its destination. At this point, it's acceptable for the ship to blow its horn. This demonstrates confidence and pride in being a well-prepared FOAMSHIP organization with a thriving soul and the ability to successfully complete all business excursions. Adopting the FOAMSHIP method ensures that a ship sails in a new way from that point on.

Focused Energy

Experience demonstrates that focus is a very powerful tool. Throughout any business passage, an organizational ship will encounter many different opportunities. Not all of these opportunities will be beneficial or aligned with the ship's specific business goals. Some will merely be distractions that could prove to be disastrous if allowed to be. Focusing resources and energy on those opportunities with the most potential is vital for the successful navigation of a ship's passage to its destination port. This maximizes the chance of achieving the organization's goals and reaping the full benefits of the enterprise.

Time, in particular, is a very limited and valuable resource that must be used wisely. Like a magnifying glass concentrating a beam of light, time must be focused on those activities that yield the highest return. This is the best

investment of an irreplaceable resource. Correctly focused energy will assist the ship in staying true to the required route and sailing smoothly along its passage.

<u>Staying the Course</u>

The ship's instrument panel, consisting of the various dashboards made up of important gauges, is utterly indispensable when it comes to monitoring the ship's progress along its passage. These gauges must be reviewed regularly to ensure that the ship remains on course.

GOALS AND OBJECTIVES

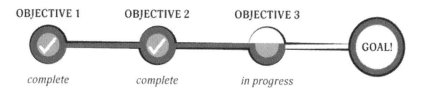

Goals and Objectives: One of the ways to confirm that an organizational ship is remaining steady in its passage is to measure the progress it has made towards achieving the predefined goals that have been set. A goal can be defined as a concise statement consisting of an expected result, and the period of time in which it should be accomplished. Business goals describe what an organization is striving to achieve, rather than how it will be done. A goal is:

- Specific
- Tangible
- Achievable
- Time-based
- Measurable
- Relevant

When setting a new goal for Bright Beacon Ltd. Sam finds it helpful to use a series of six questions to make sure that the goal is well-defined and aligned with her ship's purpose.

1. What? – is it that is to be achieved?
2. Who? – will be involved in accomplishing this goal?

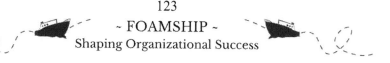

3. Why? – does this need to be done?
4. Where? – will the goal be pursued?
5. When? – is the start-point and end-point?
6. Which? – resources will be required?

Common examples of organizational goals are to increase profitability, expand the existing customer base, improve customer loyalty, enhance product quality, and explore new revenue streams.

Comparatively, an objective is an actionable component required to achieve a specific goal. Whereas a goal will describe to the crew what result needs to be achieved, the objectives are the stepping stones leading to the goalpost. For example, if the goal is to increase the organization's profit margin, one of the objectives might be to reduce the cost of overhead by 5% within 6 months. This provides the details of one specific action that can be taken towards achieving the desired result. Successfully completing this objective will constitute progress towards accomplishing the goal.

Goals and objectives are like buoys in the ocean which can be used to mark the ship's progress along its passage and measure whether it remains on course for a successful voyage.

~ FOAMSHIP ~
Shaping Organizational Success

REPUTATION

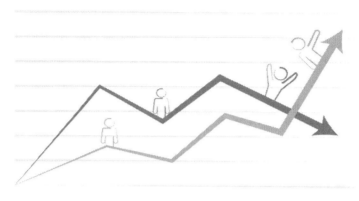

Reputation: An organization's reputation can quite literally make the difference between it sailing steadily along its passage, or sinking. Not only do many businesses not invest enough resources in cultivating and maintaining a positive reputation, but it's surprisingly common for the ship's reputation to not even be measured or monitored. Informed opinions and personal experiences can have a tremendous impact on how an organization is viewed, and whether or not it is successful.

It can take a very long time to build a strong and positive reputation, but a firm footing will enable the ship to weather the negative storms that are inevitable. Opinions, by their very nature, are typically subjective. This means that it's unrealistic to expect to prevent all negativity. It is also a simple fact that things sometimes go awry. The true test of an organization is how it handles issues that arise throughout the journey.

Monitoring and managing an organization's reputation create an environment where negative incidents are converted to positive experiences. For example, a customer is dissatisfied with the quality of a particular product and requests a refund. After investigating, it is determined that the product is indeed faulty and the customer's dissatisfaction is validated. Processing the requested refund without further delay or argument will leave the customer feeling heard, understood, and valued. It's then very likely that they may become a repeat customer because the organization has earned their trust by demonstrating an ethical and customer-centric culture. Customers generally place a greater level of importance on the resolution to a problem, than the problem itself.

Reputation does not only relate to how an organization is viewed by its customers, but also by all other parties associated with it. When a ship has a good reputation, it will attract the best crew, suppliers, investors, and partners. There are many ways to build a beneficial reputation, and these will vary from one business vessel to another. General elements to consider include:

- Establishing reputation management guidelines throughout the organization
- Creating an organizational culture that focuses on positive experiences for all
- Utilizing training, technology, and tools to manage and maintain the organization's reputation
- Proactively engage with customers, crew, and other stakeholders to manage feedback and expectations
- Promote open and smooth-flowing communication channels to ensure everyone is heard and information is shared

Monitoring and measuring reputation can help to prevent many problems from having a lasting and disproportionately negative impact. It also provides opportunities to reassure all stakeholders that they can expect a reliably positive experience when dealing with a particular ship. Testimonials, online reviews, social media engagement, and repeat customers are helpful sources of reputation data.

Sam and Fran decide to take things a step further and also create an online case library (www.foamship.com/cases) of real-life FOAMSHIP success stories. This easily-accessible trove of examples and testimonials serves to demonstrate that the FOAMSHIP approach works. Information that illustrates success will motivate and inspire the crew to embrace an environment dedicated to continuous learning and improvement.

~ FOAMSHIP ~
Shaping Organizational Success

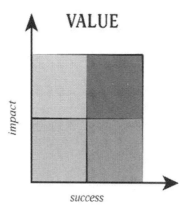

Value: Throughout all journeys, organizational success will ultimately be measured by the value that is provided to the ship's stakeholders. Measurable Organizational Value, commonly referred to as MOV, is a term attributed to Jack Marchewk, a management information systems professor. Developed as an alternative to ROI (Return on Investment), MOV considers organizational success from a different perspective.

ROI evaluates a business expedition using a comparison of profit vs. cost, whereas MOV measures the success or failure of a voyage in terms of the desired effect of the endeavor. This impact can be financial or nonfinancial and will depend on the business goals that have been set. For example, the goal may be to introduce a new line of product offerings. MOV will then define the project's value in terms of how many beneficial new products are developed and launched. This helps to focus the use of organizational resources on projects that provide the most value to the achievement of business goals.

Using the MOV method to define value offers a broader view of what constitutes value, and this can be significant in determining whether a ship is successfully traveling along its passage en route to achieve its goals. To offer real value, a business voyage must align with the ship's heading, which is a combination of vision and mission. To ensure this value is attained, the following criteria must be met:

♦ Measurability – the value of a voyage must be measurable in order to be able to determine whether or not it can be considered a success.
♦ Clarity – what constitutes a business expedition's value must be clearly defined and agreed upon.

♦ Verifiability – for the value of a business voyage to act as a measure of its success, it must be possible to verify whether the expected results were achieved.

All journeys undertaken by an organizational ship must be worth undertaking. Resources should be allocated to voyages that bring value to the organization and its stakeholders. Sometimes the value will only be reaped at a later stage of the journey, but it's important to invest in the enterprises that will steer the ship towards achieving the objectives along its passage, towards its goal.

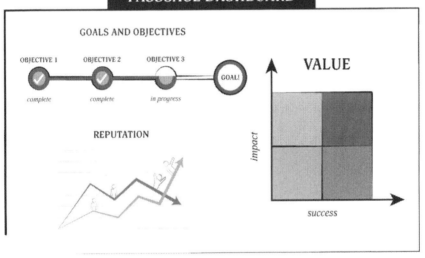

Now that every element of the FOAMSHIP method has been discovered and explored, the time has come to truly test the ship's seaworthiness on open water. Sam looks out proudly over Fran and her devoted crew as Bright Beacon Ltd. leaves the safe harbor of its home port, and sets sail towards a future full of promise and potential.

Anchors aweigh and bon voyage!

~ FOAMSHIP ~
Shaping Organizational Success

Examples: Passage

Consult the FOAMSHIP online case library (www.foamship.com/cases) to learn from extraordinary captains and hone your own captain skills. These exemplary companies offer valuable real-life guidance for navigating a ship's Passage.

Key Points: Passage

Review the key discussion points for this chapter.

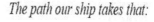

PASSAGE

The path our ship takes that:

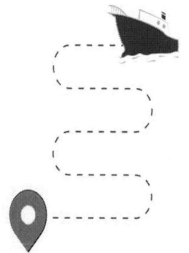

- Includes all the planned and unexpected events that could potentially affect the vessel.
- Provides unique learning experiences to bolster and increase competency and knowledge with each passage.
- Stimulates us to continuously improve our business seafaring skills.
- Adds value to the organization and its souls with each successful voyage.

~ FOAMSHIP ~
Shaping Organizational Success

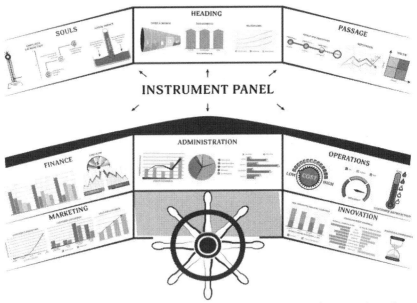

Remember to keep a close eye on your instrument panel to monitor the gauges of each FOAMSHIP component's dashboard.

Pulpit: Passage

Use these questions to hone your skills in applying the FOAMSHIP model in practice.

1. Consider each FOAMSHIP component and compile a list of ways in which you are now better prepared for your next professional voyage.
2. Compile a list of ways in which adopting the FOAMSHIP approach can better prepare you for the next leg of your personal journey.
3. Consider how you and your organization can further develop and grow using the FOAMSHIP principles.
4. Create an evolving list of self-development opportunities and goals to help you focus on continuous improvement throughout both your professional and personal expeditions.

11. CONCLUSION

"If my ship sails from sight, it doesn't mean my journey ends, it simply means the river bends."

Enoch Powell

Congratulations on completing the fundamentals of FOAMSHIP! Through our discussion of the eight FOAMSHIP components, we hope you now have a clear picture of what it takes to run a successful organizational ship. Just as visualization can help athletes perform at new heights, it can also help individuals and organizations to reach new ports.

From bow to stern, we considered the different components of any business vessel. We noted the importance of awareness in Finance and how cash serves as an organization's fuel. Too often, businesses, especially startups, fail to manage fuel supplies efficiently or figure it out too late. In Operations, delivering great products and top-notch services to Marketing's carefully selected customers maintains the ship's growth. And wise captains and officers on the Administration's bridge guide the organization and its shipmates on a fulfilling journey, come rain or shine.

But remember, without clear and effective communication, the ship is Heading nowhere fast. The FOAMSHIP approach encourages strong communication channels and ensures that all crew members see themselves as an important part of the larger whole. This motivates all those on board to actively participate in sharing information and useful knowledge. A smooth flow of information enables the constant Innovation required to keep the ship agile and competitive.

Throughout this guidebook, we have illustrated the connections and interdependencies between the business elements and human aspects of an organization. The importance of the human element, the Soul, within an organization is immeasurable. There's a growing belief that businesses should be seen as living organisms and this shines a light on the need to nurture the ship's soul in order for it to successfully travel its required Passage.

~ FOAMSHIP ~
Shaping Organizational Success

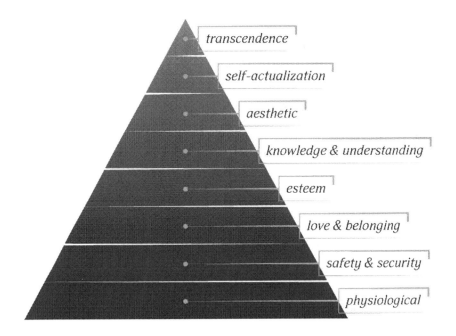

Originally consisting of 5 levels, Maslow's Hierarchy of Needs was later expanded to provide a more accurate representation of human needs and what is required to nurture the soul. This motivational theory states that the needs that are lower down in the hierarchy must be fulfilled before an individual can achieve the higher-level needs. The 8 human needs, as defined by Maslow, are:

1. *Physiological* – air, food, drink, shelter, warmth, sleep, biological needs, etc.
2. *Safety & Security* – protection from the elements, law, order, personal and professional security, freedom from fear, stability, etc.
3. *Love & Belonging* – trust, intimacy, friendship, companionship, acceptance, giving and receiving affection and love, affiliation, being part of a group (relating to friends, family, and work), etc.
4. *Esteem* – divided into two categories: esteem for oneself (independence, achievement, skill mastery, dignity, career satisfaction) and esteem from others (reputation, prestige, status, respect).
5. *Knowledge & Understanding* – curiosity, exploration, knowledge and true understanding, meaning, etc.

~ FOAMSHIP ~
Shaping Organizational Success

6. *Aesthetic* – balance, form, appreciation, and search for beauty, etc.
7. *Self-Actualization* – self-fulfillment, realizing personal potential, personal growth, professional development, experience, etc.
8. *Transcendence* – aesthetic experiences, pursuit of science, spirituality, religion, mystical experiences, service to others, the collective spirit, etc.

Supporting Maslow's theory, psychology states that an individual's feelings about work play a significant role in how they define who they are. It provides a sense of self, and feelings of worth and accomplishment. Given the importance of this, and the fact that almost half of our lives are spent working, nothing would be better than being able to truthfully say "I love what I do, and I do what I love." Yet so many individuals remain unfulfilled in their day-to-day grind. Adopting the FOAMSHIP method offers the opportunity to change this for the better and develop a more positive and satisfying working life.

As highlighted, the right environment can be highly motivating. When the working environment gives 100%, the individuals performing their roles within that environment will be more likely to give 100%. With the right culture in place, crew members will proudly perform and display their work, enjoy the environment that surrounds them, appreciate their co-workers, and strive for success. This leads to truly caring about professional growth, group productivity, and the achievement of goals. When there is a healthy balance between work, family, and community, the Soul glows.

Spending such a large portion of our lives in a working environment means that we owe it to ourselves, and those around us, to try and make it as positive as possible. Supporting and encouraging each other helps to create a culture where work can be a truly meaningful part of life. A well-led organization has the capacity to fulfill specific needs so that each individual member of the crew can reach their professional potential. Satisfying work can be highly nourishing soul food.

Being a captain isn't for everyone and this shouldn't detract from, or deny a satisfactory work experience. If organizations spent more time on bringing individuals together, they would spend far less time and money on corrective actions along the way.

The power of FOAMSHIP is in its simplicity and practicality. Whether you are a leader, a business student, an individual at a firm, an entrepreneur/intrapreneur, or simply looking to improve your professional or personal future, you can utilize the concepts here to your advantage. When working on a case at school, you can use FOAMSHIP to prompt you to review each aspect of the situation to make sure you identify the relevant factors and visualize potential situations and solutions. If you're developing a business plan for a class or a real startup, keep FOAMSHIP in mind to organize and crystallize your thoughts.

For the adventurous types chasing dreams of any kind, FOAMSHIP can be a powerful ally both professionally and personally. If you're an entrepreneur or considering this path, FOAMSHIP can help to ensure that you're making the most of your time. There will be more work than hours in the day whilst building and launching your own ship, so adopting the FOAMSHIP method will be highly beneficial. This can also help you to create the best possible crew to support your mission and assist your ship in reaching its desired destination.

Remember to take time for you and your team to focus. Share any good news that comes along. Share the bad news to mitigate its potential impact. Celebrate all victories together and lament the defeats together. Just be sure to never give up and to always bear in mind that you don't have to try and do it all alone. Go on – visualize your success and use FOAMSHIP to help you to achieve it.

Perhaps you're an intrapreneur who is more comfortable with contributing new ideas within a larger established organization. The FOAMSHIP approach can provide you with a fresh perspective as you observe current operations and suggest ideas for a more efficient business vessel. You don't have to wear as many hats as an entrepreneur and can instead focus all your energy on being innovative for the benefit of the entire crew. There is a place for everyone aboard the FOAMSHIP.

In an established business, you can also use FOAMSHIP to rethink and enhance your business model. Your entire team can take an outside-in look at the organization as a whole, break it down into the eight FOAMSHIP components, and reassemble it more effectively to provide greater value. Even mature organizations always have opportunities for rebirth. Tackling continuous improvement from this viewpoint also helps all those involved to see that all actions have an impact, so it's important to ensure the impact is as positive as possible.

~ FOAMSHIP ~
Shaping Organizational Success

Finally, don't be hesitant to implement FOAMSHIP concepts into your personal life. Your life is also a journey that needs to be navigated in the most effective manner possible. To get where you want to be, you need to manage a budget, hone necessary skills, manage your time, continuously learn and improve, and exude confidence in your abilities. As well as all this, you'll need to trust yourself and your decisions, set goals, communicate effectively, and manage uncertainty. FOAMSHIP can help you to find, and remain on, your path, feel good about your decisions, and make the most of your life so you can enjoy it.

At the core of the FOAMSHIP method, we have brought together the technical aspects of management and the needs of the individual in the organization: the need to perform with the need to belong; the need to achieve with the need to succeed; the need to nurture with the need to grow. No longer are there two incongruous forces, individual and organization, pushing and pulling in different directions. The science of management and the art of leadership have been bridged to aid a smoother journey.

You are now ready for a rewarding voyage. To travel along unexplored routes filled with exhilarating adventures and a renewed sense of purpose. Embark on your journey like Columbus or Magellan, and never lose your curiosity or desire for knowledge. If you always follow your own internal compass, you're bound to find great treasures.

We wish you many wonderful and fruitful expeditions!
Ahoy!

12. APPENDIX – FOAMSHIP SUMMARY

FINANCE

The ship's fuel tanks, where we:

- Provide value-added insight and analysis on the financial well-being of the ship.
- Ensure there is sufficient cash for those short trips and long voyages.
- Compensate and reward talented crew properly so they won't jump ship.
- Constantly look for ways to conserve fuel and protect our fuel supply (customers).

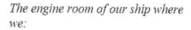

OPERATIONS

The engine room of our ship where we:

- Create the products and services which propel our ship forward.
- Use technology to build solid links with suppliers and provide added value to customers.
- Keep the crew ship-shape by providing the latest training in best practices.
- Continuously fine-tune the engine to provide efficient product and service delivery.
- Constantly monitor processes to identify improvement opportunities.

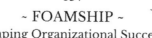

~ FOAMSHIP ~
Shaping Organizational Success

ADMINISTRATION

The bridge of our ship where:

- Our organization benefits from managerial, entrepreneurial, and intrapreneurial character profiles.
- Captains and officers complement each other's strengths and compensate for each other's weaknesses.
- The entire crew works together to maximize our ship's range.
- Captains and officers manage all the interdependencies of the FOAMSHIP components, to maintain the ship's course.
- Directives are clearly defined so everyone knows their roles and responsibilities.
- The approach to management fosters a healthy, supportive, and positive environment.

MARKETING

The compass of our ship which helps us to:

- Actively canvas the business climate to understand the wants and needs of our customers.
- Navigate the competitive battlefields to position our ship as the best choice.
- Guide our ship to relevant customer ports to provide the right products and/or services.
- Constantly create new and improved products and services to extend our ship's reach and range.
- Follow customer feedback to reach the highest levels of customer satisfaction.

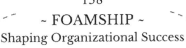 ~ FOAMSHIP ~
Shaping Organizational Success

SOULS

The collective human energy aboard our ship that:

- Provides rational and analytical capabilities, as well as intuitive and creative genius.
- Gives the organization meaning and links people to purpose.
- Can be cultivated to be a tremendous source of innovative ideas.
- Is a direct reflection of our most differentiating asset – our people's spirit.

HEADING

The bright star on the horizon that:

- Is palpable and embraceable by all crew members.
- Provides a clear sense of direction.
- Unites the captain and crew through a shared vision.
- Focuses the energies of all crew members on a common destination.
- Needs to be communicated throughout the voyage to keep crew members aligned.
- Provides reassuring clarity to customers, suppliers, partners, and investors.

~ FOAMSHIP ~
Shaping Organizational Success

INNOVATION

Our ship's ability to innovate:

- Facilitates the flow of information and the sharing of data throughout the organization.
- Enables effective communication between captains, officers, and shipmates at all levels.
- Captures valuable knowledge for future journeys, thus increasing organizational learning and information-sharing.

PASSAGE

The path our ship takes that:

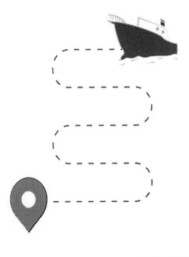

- Includes all the planned and unexpected events that could potentially affect the vessel.
- Provides unique learning experiences to bolster and increase competency and knowledge with each passage.
- Stimulates us to continuously improve our business seafaring skills.
- Adds value to the organization and its souls with each successful voyage.

~ FOAMSHIP ~
Shaping Organizational Success

13. BIBLIOGRAPHY

1. Ailes, R. & Kraushar, J. (1995). You are the message: Getting what you want by being who you are. Currency/Doubleday.
2. America, R. F. & Anderson, B. E. (1997). Soul in Management: How African-American Managers Thrive in the Competitive Corporate Environment. Citadel Press.
3. Bandura, A. (1997). Self-Efficacy: The Exercise of Control. W.H. Freeman & Co.
4. Benton, D.A. (1994). Lions Don't Need to Roar: Using the Leadership Power of Professional Presence to Stand Out, Fit in and Move Ahead. Warner Books.
5. Benton, D.A. (1996). How to Think Like a CEO: The 22 Vital Traits You Need to Be the Person at the Top. Warner Books.
6. Brigham, E. F. & Gapenski, L. C. (1994). Financial Management: Theory and Practice, 7th Edition. Harcourt Brace.
7. Case, J. (1997). What You Can Learn from Open-Book Management. Harvard Management Update, 2 (12), 1-4.
8. Cooper, R. K. & Sawaf, Ayman (1997). Executive EQ: Emotional Intelligence in Leadership and Organizations. Putnam Publishing Group.
9. Copeland, T.; Koller, T.; Murvin, J. (1990). Valuation: Measuring and Managing the Value of Companies. John Wiley & Sons.
10. Covey, S. R. (1990). The 7 Habits of Highly Effective People: Powerful Lessons in Personal Change. Fireside.
11. Covey, S. R. (1992). Principle-Centered Leadership. Fireside.
12. Covey, S. R.; Merrill, A. R.; Merrill, R. (1996). First Things First: To Live, to Love, to Learn, to Leave a Legacy. Fireside.
13. Cox, A. J.; Liesse, J.; Cox, A. (1996). Redefining Corporate Soul: Linking People and Purpose. Irwin Professional Publishing.
14. Drucker, P. F. (1993). Innovation and Entrepreneurship: Practice and Principles. Harper Business.
15. Envick, B. R. & Langford, M. (2000). The Five-Factor Model of Personality: Assessing Entrepreneurs and Managers. Academy of Entrepreneurship Journal, Volume 6, Number 1, 2000, 6-17.
16. Drucker, P. F. (1993). Managing for the Future: The 1990s and Beyond. Plume.
17. Goldratt, E. & Cox, J. (1994). The Goal: A Process of Ongoing Improvement. North River Press.
18. Goleman, D. (1995). Emotional Intelligence. Bantam Books.
19. Gordon, T. Dr. (1997). Leader Effectiveness Training, L.E.T.: The

~ FOAMSHIP ~
Shaping Organizational Success

Foundation for Participative Management and Employee Involvement. Putnam Publishing Group.
20. Hamel, G. & Prahalad, C. K. (1996). Competing for the Future. Harvard Business School Press.
21. Heskett, J. L.; Sasser, W. E.; Schlesinger, L. A. (1997). The Service Profit Chain: How Leading Companies Link Profit and Growth to Loyalty, Satisfaction and Value. Free Press.
22. Horngren, Ch. T.; Sunden, G. L.; Elliot, J. A. (1993). Introduction to Financial Accounting, 5th Edition. Prentice-Hall.
23. Jacobs, J. (1997). Navigating the Waters. Update: Kenan-Flagler Business School, Spring 1997, 5.
24. Jaworski, J. (1996). Synchronicity: The Inner Path of Leadership. Berrett-Koehler Publishing.
25. Jones, L. B. (1996). Jesus CEO: Using Ancient Wisdom for Visionary Leadership. Hyperion.
26. Klein, E. & Izzo, J. B. (1997). Awakening Corporate Soul: 4 Paths to Unleash the Power of People at Work. Fair Winds Press.
27. Kotler, P. (1994). Marketing Management: Analysis, Planning, Implementation and Control. Prentice-Hall.
28. Kotter, J. P. (1990). Force for Change: How Leadership Differs from Management. Free Press.
29. Kotter, J. P. & Heskett, J. L. (1992). Corporate Culture and Performance. Free Press.
30. Kotter, J. P. (1995). The New Rules: How to succeed in today's Post-Corporate World. Free Press.
31. Kotter, J. P. (1996). Leading Change. Harvard Business School Press.
32. Lawhon, J. F. (1995). The Selling Bible for People in the Business of Selling. J. Franklin Publishers.
33. Marchand, R. (1998). Creating the Corporate Soul: The Rise of Public Relations and Corporate Imagery in American Big Business. University California Press.
34. Normann, R. & Ramirez, R. (1994). Designing Interactive Strategy: From Value Chain to Value Constellation. John Wiley & Sons.
35. Peters, T. (1991). Thriving on Chaos: Handbook for a Management Revolution. Harper Collins.
36. Peter, T. (1994). Liberation Management: Necessary Disorganization for the Nanosecond Nineties. Fawcett Books.
37. Peters, T. (1994). The Pursuit of Wow!: Every Person's Guide to Topsy-Turvy Times. Vintage Books.
38. Pfeffer, J. (1998). The Human Equation: Building Profits by Putting

~ FOAMSHIP ~
Shaping Organizational Success

People First. Harvard Business School Press.

39. Ries, A. & Trout, J. (1994). The 22 Immutable Laws of Marketing: Violate Them at Your Own Risk. Harper Business.

40. Senge, P. M. (1990). The Fifth Discipline: The Art and Practice of the Learning Organization. Currency/Doubleday.

41. Walmsley, A. (1997). Six Sigma Enigmas. Report on Business Magazine, October 1997, 1-7.

42. Webster, F. E. (1994). Market-Driven Management: Using the New Marketing Concept to Create a Customer-Oriented Company. John Wiley & Sons.

43. Whyte, D. (1994). The Heart Aroused: Poetry and the Preservation of the Soul in Corporate America. Currency/Doubleday.

14. ABOUT THE AUTHORS

Mr. R. David Bermudez is a professional engineer with a Bachelor in Electrical & Computer Engineering from the University of Notre Dame and a Master's in Business Administration from the University of North Carolina at Chapel Hill. He is currently President of Onopa Services, a federal construction firm with projects across multiple states. He is also the Founder of TECODE, a non-profit organization focused on technology, environment, and community development.

Mr. J. R. Lluberas spent the first half of his career in tech, consulting, and venture capital, where he helped entities become more competitive by increasing the efficiency of their operations through business process improvement techniques, engaging in strategic partnerships, and tapping into the soul of management. Now in the second act of his working life, he is dedicated to nonprofits and philanthropy. Like David, he also holds Engineering and Business degrees, both from Northeastern University in Boston.

TESTIMONIALS FROM EARLIER EDITIONS

"Peak individual and organizational performance requires an integration of both the rational and emotional faculties of the human mind. Individuals with highly developed emotional intelligence can build visionary organizations that sense today's challenges and create tomorrow's opportunities. The FOAMSHIP is an intuitive and practical model that can be useful to visualize and steer business organizations riding the high seas."

Dr. Robert K Cooper, Author of *"The Performance Edge"* and *"Executive EQ: Emotional Intelligence in Business"*

"As Antoine de Saint-Exupery helped us to understand the world through simple words and imaginary anecdotes in the 1943 book "The Little Prince", the authors have brought new light – a new vision to the wonders of innovative business management with "THE FOAMSHIP". Running through its pages is so easy, like gossip in a classroom, that to fully appreciate its wisdom it takes several readings."

Jimmy Sotomayor Lopez, University Professor

www.foamship.com

~ FOAMSHIP ~
Shaping Organizational Success

Made in the USA
Columbia, SC
02 June 2021

38533316R00087